the
poetry
of
W.B.Yeats

ISBN
9781788287760

W0008624

the
poetry
of
W.B.Yeats

This edition published in 2019 by Arcturus Publishing Limited
26/27 Bickels Yard, 151–153 Bermondsey Street,
London SE1 3HA

Copyright © Arcturus Holdings Limited

All rights reserved. No part of this publication may be reproduced,
stored in a retrieval system, or transmitted, in any form or by any
means, electronic, mechanical, photocopying, recording or otherwise,
without prior written permission in accordance with the provisions of
the Copyright Act 1956 (as amended). Any person or persons who do
any unauthorised act in relation to this publication may be liable to
criminal prosecution and civil claims for damages.

AD006343UK

Printed in the UK

Contents

Introduction

William Butler Yeats is regarded as one of the greatest poets of the 20th century. His lifetime spanned two artistic movements, the Victorian era and Modernism, the conflicting currents of which affected his work, both of which are featured in this wide-ranging collection of his poetry. He was an artist in the true sense of the word, studying painting, before mastering the art of poetry and becoming a major playwright and one of the founders of the famous Abbey Theatre in Dublin.

He was born in Dublin in 1865. His father, John Butler Yeats, was a well-known Irish painter, and his mother Susan Mary Pollexfen came from a family of merchants in Sligo. The family belonged to the Anglo-Irish Protestant minority that had controlled the economic, political, social and cultural life in Ireland since the end of the 17th century. Most members of this minority considered themselves English people who happened to have been born in Ireland, but as he grew up Yeats was increasingly keen to affirm his Irish nationality.

When William was two, the family moved to London where they remained for 14 years, before returning to Dublin in 1881. William studied at the Metropolitan School of Art and quickly discovered that he preferred poetry. His first collection was published in 1889. The poems pursued themes that were to remain central to his writing – Ireland, its legends and folklore, spiritualism and love. By this time back in London, he met and fell in love with Maud Gonne, an Irishwoman equally famous for her passionate nationalist politics and her beauty. She served as his muse for years, further inspiring his nationalism by hers and his poetry by her rejection of his advances, though he would pursue her for the next three decades.

Yeats continued to pursue his other interests, too. In 1890, he helped set up the Rhymers' Club, a group of poets who met at the Cheshire Cheese pub in Fleet Street to recite and discuss their work, and joined the Golden Dawn, a secret society that practised ritual magic. Scholars believe that both these activities helped Yeats refine his poetic style.

In 1896, Yeats was introduced to the Irish dramatist Lady

Gregory by their mutual friend Edward Martyn. Yeats had written a number of successful 'nationalistic' plays in the early 1890s, and Gregory encouraged Yeats's nationalism, and convinced him to focus on writing drama. This led to the founding of the Irish National Theatre Society. With a wealthy sponsor paying for the renovation of Dublin's Abbey Theatre as its permanent home, the society opened its doors in December 1904, and staged plays by Gregory and Yeats.

He continued to write poetry, and his style developed during the early years of the new century, no doubt influenced by his playwriting. Still retaining their traditional verse forms, symbolism and energy, they engage with the complexities of life, but Yeats also wanted them to be simpler, as if he was 'walking naked' as he says in his poem 'A Coat', written in 1912. Gone was the pleasant musicality of 'The Lake Isle of Innisfree', written twenty years earlier.

Finally admitting that neither Maud Gonne nor her daughter Iseult, for whom he also had romantic inclinations, were to be in his future, in 1917, he married Georgie Hyde-Lees with whom he had two children.

The political situation in Ireland in the post-war years was fraught with bitter controversy over the Irish Free State and the partition of Northern Ireland. Siding firmly with the Irish government, Yeats became involved politically, serving as a senator for six years, beginning in 1922. The following year, he was awarded the Nobel Prize in Literature 'for his always inspired poetry, which in a highly artistic form gives expression to the spirit of a whole nation.'

The poems and plays that Yeats produced during these disturbing times gave astonishing power to his collection *The Tower* (1928), which is often considered his best single book.

When Yeats was nearly 60, his health began to fail and he was faced with real, rather than imaginary, 'bodily decrepitude'. Despite this, the last 15 years of his life were marked by extraordinary vitality and an appetite for life. He continued to write until his death in late January 1939.

The Song of the Happy Shepherd

The woods of Arcady are dead,
And over is their antique joy;
Of old the world on dreaming fed;
Grey Truth is now her painted toy;
Yet still she turns her restless head:
But O, sick children of the world,
Of all the many changing things
In dreary dancing past us whirled,
To the cracked tune that Chronos sings,
Words alone are certain good.
Where are now the warring kings,
Word be-mockers? − By the Rood,
Where are now the warring kings?
An idle word is now their glory,
By the stammering schoolboy said,
Reading some entangled story:
The kings of the old time are dead;
The wandering earth herself may be
Only a sudden flaming word,
In clanging space a moment heard,
Troubling the endless reverie.

Then nowise worship dusty deeds,
Nor seek, for this is also sooth,
To hunger fiercely after truth,
Lest all thy toiling only breeds
New dreams, new dreams; there is no truth
Saving in thine own heart. Seek, then,
No learning from the starry men,
Who follow with the optic glass
The whirling ways of stars that pass −

Seek, then, for this is also sooth,
No word of theirs — the cold star-bane
Has cloven and rent their hearts in twain,
And dead is all their human truth.
Go gather by the humming sea
Some twisted, echo-harbouring shell,
And to its lips thy story tell,
And they thy comforters will be,
Rewording in melodious guile
Thy fretful words a little while,
Till they shall singing fade in ruth
And die a pearly brotherhood;
For words alone are certain good:
Sing, then, for this is also sooth.

I must be gone: there is a grave
Where daffodil and lily wave,
And I would please the hapless faun,
Buried under the sleepy ground,
With mirthful songs before the dawn.
His shouting days with mirth were crowned;
And still I dream he treads the lawn,
Walking ghostly in the dew,
Pierced by my glad singing through,
My songs of old earth's dreamy youth:
But ah! she dreams not now; dream thou!
For fair are poppies on the brow:
Dream, dream, for this is also sooth.

The Cloak, the Boat and the Shoes

'What do you make so fair and bright?'

'I make the cloak of Sorrow:
O lovely to see in all men's sight
Shall be the cloak of Sorrow,
In all men's sight.'

'What do you build with sails for flight?'

'I build a boat for Sorrow:
O swift on the seas all day and night
Saileth the rover Sorrow,
All day and night.'

'What do you weave with wool so white?'

'I weave the shoes of Sorrow:
Soundless shall be the footfall light
In all men's ears of Sorrow,
Sudden and light.'

Anashuya and Vijaya

A little Indian temple in the Golden Age. Around it a garden; around that the forest. Anashuya, the young priestess, kneeling within the temple.

Anashuya. Send peace on all the lands and flickering
    corn —
  O, may tranquillity walk by his elbow
  When wandering in the forest, if he love
  No other. — Hear, and may the indolent flocks
  Be plentiful. — And if he love another,
  May panthers end him. — Hear, and load our king
  With wisdom hour by hour. — May we two stand,
  When we are dead, beyond the setting suns,
  A little from the other shades apart,
  With mingling hair, and play upon one lute.

Vijaya [*entering and throwing a lily at her*]. Hail! hail, my
    Anashuya.

Anashuya. No: be still.
  I, priestess of this temple, offer up
  prayers for the land.

Vijaya. I will wait here, Amrita.

Anashuya. By mighty Brahma's ever-rustling robe,
  Who is Amrita? Sorrow of all sorrows!
  Another fills your mind.

Vijaya. My mother's name.

Anashuya [*sings, coming out of the temple*].

    A sad, sad thought went by me slowly:

    Sigh, O you little stars.! O sigh and shake your blue apparel!

    The sad, sad thought has gone from me now wholly:

    Sing, O you little stars.! O sing and raise your rapturous carol

    To mighty Brahma, he who made you many as the sands,

    And laid you on the gates of evening with his quiet hands.

                [*sits down on the steps of the temple.*]

    Vijaya, I have brought my evening rice;

    The sun has laid his chin on the grey wood,

    Weary, with all his poppies gathered round him.

Vijaya. The hour when Kama, full of sleepy laughter,

    Rises, and showers abroad his fragrant arrows,

    Piercing the twilight with their murmuring barbs.

Anashuya. See how the sacred old flamingoes come.

    Painting with shadow all the marble steps:

    Aged and wise, they seek their wonted perches

    Within the temple, devious walking, made

    To wander by their melancholy minds.

    Yon tall one eyes my supper; chase him away,

    Far, far away. I named him after you.

    He is a famous fisher; hour by hour

    He ruffles with his bill the minnowed streams.

    Ah! there he snaps my rice. I told you so.

    Now cuff him off. He's off! A kiss for you,

    Because you saved my rice. Have you no thanks?

Vijaya [*sings*]. *Sing you of her, O first few stars,*

    Whom Brahma, touching with his finger, praises, for you hold

    The van of wandering quiet; ere you be too calm and old,

    Sing, turning in your cars,

Sing, till you raise your hands and sigh, and from your car-heads peer,
With all your whirling hair, and drop many an azure tear.

Anashuya. What know the pilots of the stars of tears?

Vijaya. Their faces are all worn, and in their eyes
 Flashes the fire of sadness, for they see
 The icicles that famish all the North,
 Where men lie frozen in the glimmering snow;
 And in the flaming forests cower the lion
 And lioness, with all their whimpering cubs;
 And, ever pacing on the verge of things,
 The phantom, Beauty, in a mist of tears;
 While we alone have round us woven woods,
 And feel the softness of each other's hand,
 Amrita, while —

Anashuya [going away from him].
 Ah me! you love another,

                              [Bursting into tears.]
 And may some sudden dreadful ill befall her!

Vijaya. I loved another; now I love no other.
 Among the mouldering of ancient woods
 You live, and on the village border she,
 With her old father the blind wood-cutter;
 I saw her standing in her door but now.

Anashuya. Vijaya, swear to love her never more.

Vijaya. Ay, ay.

Anashuya. Swear by the parents of the gods,

Dread oath, who dwell on sacred Himalay,
On the far Golden Peak; enormous shapes,
Who still were old when the great sea was young;
On their vast faces mystery and dreams;
Their hair along the mountains rolled and filled
From year to year by the unnumbered nests
Of aweless birds, and round their stirless feet
The joyous flocks of deer and antelope,
Who never hear the unforgiving hound.
Swear!

Vijaya. By the parents of the gods, I swear.

Anashuya [sings]. *I have forgiven, O new star!*
Maybe you have not heard of us, you have come forth so newly,
You hunter of the fields afar!
Ah, you will know my loved one by his hunter's arrows truly,
Shoot on him shafts of quietness, that he may ever keep
A lonely laughter, and may kiss his hands to me in sleep.

Farewell, Vijaya. Nay, no word, no word;
I, priestess of this temple, offer up
Prayers for the land.
                              [*Vijaya goes.*]
                    O Brahma, guard in sleep
The merry lambs and the complacent kine,
The flies below the leaves, and the young mice
In the tree roots, and all the sacred flocks
Of red flamingoes; and my love, Vijaya;
And may no restless fay with fidget finger
Trouble his sleeping: give him dreams of me.

The Indian to His Love

The island dreams under the dawn
And great boughs drop tranquillity;
The peahens dance on a smooth lawn,
A parrot sways upon a tree,
Raging at his own image in the enamelled sea.

Here we will moor our lonely ship
And wander ever with woven hands,
Murmuring softly lip to lip,
Along the grass, along the sands,
Murmuring how far away are the unquiet lands:

How we alone of mortals are
Hid under quiet boughs apart,
While our love grows an Indian star,
A meteor of the burning heart,
One with the tide that gleams, the wings that
   gleam and dart,

The heavy boughs, the burnished dove
That moans and sighs a hundred days:
How when we die our shades will rove,
When eve has hushed the feathered ways,
With vapoury footsole by the water's drowsy blaze.

Ephemera

'Your eyes that once were never weary of mine
Are bowed in sorrow under pendulous lids,
Because our love is waning.'
                              And then she:
'Although our love is waning, let us stand
By the long border of the lake once more,
Together in that hour of gentleness
When the poor tired child, Passion, falls asleep:
How far away the stars seem, and how far
Is our first kiss, and ah, how old my heart!'
Pensive they paced along the faded leaves,
While slowly he whose hand held hers replied:
'Passion has often worn our wandering hearts.'

The woods were round them, and the yellow leaves
Fell like faint meteors in the gloom, and once
A rabbit old and lame limped down the path;
Autumn was over him: and now they stood
On the lone border of the lake once more:
Turning, he saw that she had thrust dead leaves
Gathered in silence, dewy as her eyes,
In bosom and hair.
                    'Ah, do not mourn,' he said,
'That we are tired, for other loves await us;
Hate on and love through unrepining hours.
Before us lies eternity; our souls
Are love, and a continual farewell.'

The Madness of King Goll

I sat on cushioned otter-skin:
My word was law from Ith to Emain,
And shook at Inver Amergin
The hearts of the world-troubling seamen,
And drove tumult and war away
From girl and boy and man and beast;
The fields grew fatter day by day,
The wild fowl of the air increased;
And every ancient Ollave said,
While he bent down his fading head,
'He drives away the Northern cold.'
They will not hush, the leaves a-flutter round me, the beech leaves old.

I sat and mused and drank sweet wine;
A herdsman came from inland valleys,
Crying, the pirates drove his swine
To fill their dark-beaked hollow galleys.
I called my battle-breaking men
And my loud brazen battle-cars
From rolling vale and rivery glen;
And under the blinking of the stars
Fell on the pirates by the deep,
And hurled them in the gulph of sleep:
These hands won many a torque of gold.
They will not hush, the leaves a-flutter round me, the beech leaves old.

But slowly, as I shouting slew
And trampled in the bubbling mire,
In my most secret spirit grew
A whirling and a wandering fire:
I stood: keen stars above me shone,

Around me shone keen eyes of men:
I laughed aloud and hurried on
By rocky shore and rushy fen;
I laughed because birds fluttered by,
And starlight gleamed, and clouds flew high,
And rushes waved and waters rolled.
They will not hush, the leaves a-flutter round me, the beech leaves old.

And now I wander in the woods
When summer gluts the golden bees,
Or in autumnal solitudes
Arise the leopard-coloured trees;
Or when along the wintry strands
The cormorants shiver on their rocks;
I wander on, and wave my hands,
And sing, and shake my heavy locks.
The grey wolf knows me; by one ear
I lead along the woodland deer;
The hares run by me growing bold.
They will not hush, the leaves a-flutter round me, the Beech leaves old.

I came upon a little town
That slumbered in the harvest moon,
And passed a-tiptoe up and down,
Murmuring, to a fitful tune,
How I have followed, night and day,
A tramping of tremendous feet,
And saw where this old tympan lay
Deserted on a doorway seat,
And bore it to the woods with me;
Of some inhuman misery
Our married voices wildly trolled.
They will not hush, the leaves a-flutter round me, the beech leaves old.

I sang how, when day's toil is done,
Orchil shakes out her long dark hair
That hides away the dying sun
And sheds faint odours through the air:
When my hand passed from wire to wire
It quenched, with sound like falling dew,
The whirling and the wandering fire;
But lift a mournful ulalu,
For the kind wires are torn and still,
And I must wander wood and hill
Through summer's heat and winter's cold.
They will not hush, the leaves a-flutter round me, the beech leaves old.

The Stolen Child

Where dips the rocky highland
Of Sleuth Wood in the lake,
There lies a leafy island
Where flapping herons wake
The drowsy water-rats;
There we've hid our faery vats,
Full of berries
And of reddest stolen cherries.
Come away, O human child!
To the waters and the wild
With a faery, hand in hand,
For the world's more full of weeping than you can understand.

Where the wave of moonlight glosses
The dim grey sands with light,
Far off by furthest Rosses
We foot it all the night,
Weaving olden dances,
Mingling hands and mingling glances
Till the moon has taken flight;
To and fro we leap
And chase the frothy bubbles,
While the world is full of troubles
And is anxious in its sleep.
Come away, O human child!
To the waters and the wild
With a faery, hand in hand,
For the world's more full of weeping than you can understand.

Where the wandering water gushes
From the hills above Glen-Car,.
In pools among the rushes
That scarce could bathe a star,
We seek for slumbering trout
And whispering in their ears
Give them unquiet dreams;
Leaning softly out
From ferns that drop their tears
Over the young streams.
Come away, O human child!
To the waters and the wild
With a faery, hand in hand,
For the world's more full of weeping than you can understand.

Away with us he's going,
The solemn-eyed:
He'll hear no more the lowing
Of the calves on the warm hillside
Or the kettle on the hob
Sing peace into his breast,
Or see the brown mice bob
Round and round the oatmeal-chest.
For he comes, the human child,
To the waters and the wild
With a faery, hand in hand,
From a world more full of weeping than he can understand.

To an Isle in the Water

Shy one, shy one,
Shy one of my heart,
She moves in the firelight
Pensively apart.

She carries in the dishes,
And lays them in a row.
To an isle in the water
With her would I go.

She carries in the candles,
And lights the curtained room,
Shy in the doorway
And shy in the gloom;

And shy as a rabbit,
Helpful and shy.
To an isle in the water
With her would I fly.

Down by the Salley Gardens

Down by the salley gardens my love and I did meet;
She passed the salley gardens with little snow-white feet.
She bid me take love easy, as the leaves grow on the tree;
But I, being young and foolish, with her would not agree.

In a field by the river my love and I did stand,
And on my leaning shoulder she laid her snow-white
  hand.
She bid me take life easy, as the grass grows on the weirs;
But I was young and foolish, and now am full of tears.

The Ballad of the Foxhunter

'Lay me in a cushioned chair;
Carry me, ye four,
With cushions here and cushions there,
To see the world once more.

'To stable and to kennel go;
Bring what is there to bring;
Lead my Lollard to and fro,
Or gently in a ring.

'put the chair upon the grass:
Bring Rody and his hounds,
That I may contented pass
From these earthly bounds.'

His eyelids droop, his head falls low,
His old eyes cloud with dreams;
The sun upon all things that grow
Falls in sleepy streams.

Brown Lollard treads upon the lawn,
And to the armchair goes,
And now the old man's dreams are gone,
He smooths the long brown nose.

And now moves many a pleasant tongue
Upon his wasted hands,
For leading aged hounds and young
The huntsman near him stands.

'Huntsman Rody, blow the horn,
Make the hills reply.'
The huntsman loosens on the morn
A gay wandering cry.

Fire is in the old man's eyes,
His fingers move and sway,
And when the wandering music dies
They hear him feebly say,

'Huntsman Rody, blow the horn,
Make the hills reply.'
'I cannot blow upon my horn,
I can but weep and sigh.'

Setvants round his cushioned place
Are with new sorrow wrung;
Hounds are gazing on his face,
Aged hounds and young.

One blind hound only lies apart
On the sun-smitten grass;
He holds deep commune with his heart:
The moments pass and pass;

The blind hound with a mournful din
Lifts slow his wintry head;
The servants bear the body in;
The hounds wail for the dead.

To the Rose upon the Rood of Time

Red Rose, proud Rose, sad Rose of all my days!
Come near me, while I sing the ancient ways:
Cuchulain battling with the bitter tide;
The Druid, grey, wood-nurtured, quiet-eyed,
Who cast round Fergus dreams, and ruin untold;
And thine own sadness, whereof stars, grown old
In dancing silver-sandalled on the sea,
Sing in their high and lonely melody.
Come near, that no more blinded by man's fate,
I find under the boughs of love and hate,
In all poor foolish things that live a day,
Eternal beauty wandering on her way.

Come near, come near, come near – Ah, leave me still
A little space for the rose-breath to fill!
Lest I no more hear common things that crave;
The weak worm hiding down in its small cave,
The field-mouse running by me in the grass,
And heavy mortal hopes that toil and pass;
But seek alone to hear the strange things said
By God to the bright hearts of those long dead,
And learn to chaunt a tongue men do not know.
Come near; I would, before my time to go,
Sing of old Eire and the ancient ways:
Red Rose, proud Rose, sad Rose of all my days.

The Rose of the World

Who dreamed that beauty passes like a dream?
For these red lips, with all their mournful pride,
Mournful that no new wonder may betide,
Troy passed away in one high funeral gleam,
And Usna's children died.

We and the labouring world are passing by:
Amid men's souls, that waver and give place
Like the pale waters in their wintry race,
Under the passing stars, foam of the sky,
Lives on this lonely face.

Bow down, archangels, in your dim abode:
Before you were, or any hearts to beat,
Weary and kind one lingered by His seat;
He made the world to be a grassy road
Before her wandering feet.

The Rose of Peace

If Michael, leader of God's host
When Heaven and Hell are met,
Looked down on you from Heaven's door-post
He would his deeds forget.

Brooding no more upon God's wars
In his divine homestead,
He would go weave out of the stars
A chaplet for your head.

And all folk seeing him bow down,
And white stars tell your praise,
Would come at last to God's great town,
Led on by gentle ways;

And God would bid his warfare cease.
Saying all things were well;
And softly make a rosy peace,
A peace of Heaven with Hell.

The Rose of Battle

Rose of all Roses, Rose of all the World!
The tall thought-woven sails, that flap unfurled
Above the tide of hours, trouble the air,
And God's bell buoyed to be the water's care;
While hushed from fear, or loud with hope, a band
With blown, spray-dabbled hair gather at hand.
Turn if you may from battles never done,
I call, as they go by me one by one,
Danger no refuge holds, and war no peace,
For him who hears love sing and never cease,
Beside her clean-swept hearth, her quiet shade:
But gather all for whom no love hath made
A woven silence, or but came to cast
A song into the air, and singing passed
To smile on the pale dawn; and gather you
Who have sought more than is in rain or dew,
Or in the sun and moon, or on the earth,
Or sighs amid the wandering, starry mirth,
Or comes in laughter from the sea's sad lips,
And wage God's battles in the long grey ships.
The sad, the lonely, the insatiable,
To these Old Night shall all her mystery tell;
God's bell has claimed them by the little cry
Of their sad hearts, that may not live nor die.

Rose of all Roses, Rose of all the World!
You, too, have come where the dim tides are hurled
Upon the wharves of sorrow, and heard ring
The bell that calls us on; the sweet far thing.
Beauty grown sad with its eternity
Made you of us, and of the dim grey sea.

Our long ships loose thought-woven sails and wait,
For God has bid them share an equal fate;
And when at last, defeated in His wars,
They have gone down under the same white stars,
We shall no longer hear the little cry
Of our sad hearts, that may not live nor die.

The Lake Isle of Innisfree

I will arise and go now, and go to Innisfree,
And a small cabin build there, of clay and wattles made:
Nine bean-rows will I have there, a hive for the
   honey-bee,
And live alone in the bee-loud glade.

And I shall have some peace there, for peace comes
   dropping slow,
Dropping from the veils of the morning to where the
   cricket sings;
There midnight's all a glimmer, and noon a purple glow,
And evening full of the linnet's wings.

I will arise and go now, for always night and day
I hear lake water lapping with low sounds by the shore;
While I stand on the roadway, or on the pavements grey,
I hear it in the deep heart's core.

A Cradle Song

The angels are stooping
Above your bed;
They weary of trooping
With the whimpering dead.

God's laughing in Heaven
To see you so good;
The Sailing Seven
Are gay with His mood.

I sigh that kiss you,
For I must own
That I shall miss you
When you are grown.

The Sorrow of Love

The brawling of a sparrow in the eaves,
The brilliant moon and all the milky sky,
And all that famous harmony of leaves,
Had blotted out man's image and his cry.

A girl arose that had red mournful lips
And seemed the greatness of the world in tears,
Doomed like Odysseus and the labouring ships
And proud as Priam murdered with his peers;

Arose, and on the instant clamorous eaves,
A climbing moon upon an empty sky,
And all that lamentation of the leaves,
Could but compose man's image and his cry.

When You are Old

When you are old and grey and full of sleep,
And nodding by the fire, take down this book,
And slowly read, and dream of the soft look
Your eyes had once, and of their shadows deep;

How many loved your moments of glad grace,
And loved your beauty with love false or true,
But one man loved the pilgrim soul in you,
And loved the sorrows of your changing face;

And bending down beside the glowing bars,
Murmur, a little sadly, how Love fled
And paced upon the mountains overhead
And hid his face amid a crowd of stars.

The White Birds

I would that we were, my beloved, white birds on the
   foam of the sea!
We tire of the flame of the meteor, before it can fade and
   flee;
And the flame of the blue star of twilight, hung low on
   the rim of the sky,
Has awakened in our hearts, my beloved, a sadness that
   may not die.

A weariness comes from those dreamers, dew-dabbled,
   the lily and rose;
Ah, dream not of them, my beloved, the flame of the
   meteor that goes,
Or the flame of the blue star that lingers hung low in the
   fall of the dew:
For I would we were changed to white birds on the
   wandering foam: I and you!

I am haunted by numberless islands, and many a Danaan
   shore,
Where Time would surely forget us, and Sorrow come
   near us no more;
Soon far from the rose and the lily, and fret of the flames
   would we be,
Were we only white birds, my beloved, buoyed out on
   the foam of the sea!

A Dream of Death

I dreamed that one had died in a strange place
Near no accustomed hand;
And they had nailed the boards above her face,
The peasants of that land,
Wondering to lay her in that solitude,
And raised above her mound
A cross they had made out of two bits of wood,
And planted cypress round;
And left her to the indifferent stars above
Until I carved these words:
She was more beautiful than thy first love,
But now lies under boards.

The Countess Cathleen in Paradise

All the heavy days are over;
Leave the body's coloured pride
Underneath the grass and clover,
With the feet laid side by side.

Bathed in flaming founts of duty
She'll not ask a haughty dress;
Carry all that mournful beauty
To the scented oaken press.

Did the kiss of Mother Mary
Put that music in her face?
Yet she goes with footstep wary,
Full of earth's old timid grace.

'Mong the feet of angels seven
What a dancer glimmering!
All the heavens bow down to Heaven,
Flame to flame and wing to wing.

Who Goes with Fergus?

Who will go drive with Fergus now,
And pierce the deep wood's woven shade,
And dance upon the level shore?
Young man, lift up your russet brow,
And lift your tender eyelids, maid,
And brood on hopes and fear no more.

And no more turn aside and brood
Upon love's bitter mystery;
For Fergus rules the brazen cars,
And rules the shadows of the wood,
And the white breast of the dim sea
And all dishevelled wandering stars.

The Man who Dreamed of Faeryland

He stood among a crowd at Dromahair;
His heart hung all upon a silken dress,
And he had known at last some tenderness,
Before earth took him to her stony care;
But when a man poured fish into a pile,
It seemed they raised their little silver heads,
And sang what gold morning or evening sheds
Upon a woven world-forgotten isle
Where people love beside the ravelled seas;
That Time can never mar a lover's vows
Under that woven changeless roof of boughs:
The singing shook him out of his new ease.

He wandered by the sands of Lissadell;
His mind ran all on money cares and fears,
And he had known at last some prudent years
Before they heaped his grave under the hill;
But while he passed before a plashy place,
A lug-worm with its grey and muddy mouth
Sang that somewhere to north or west or south
There dwelt a gay, exulting, gentle race
Under the golden or the silver skies;
That if a dancer stayed his hungry foot
It seemed the sun and moon were in the fruit:
And at that singing he was no more wise.

He mused beside the well of Scanavin,
He mused upon his mockers: without fail
His sudden vengeance were a country tale,
When earthy night had drunk his body in;
But one small knot-grass growing by the pool

Sang where — unnecessary cruel voice —
Old silence bids its chosen race rejoice,
Whatever ravelled waters rise and fall
Or stormy silver fret the gold of day,
And midnight there enfold them like a fleece
And lover there by lover be at peace.
The tale drove his fine angry mood away.

He slept under the hill of Lugnagall;
And might have known at last unhaunted sleep
Under that cold and vapour-turbaned steep,
Now that the earth had taken man and all:
Did not the worms that spired about his bones
Proclaim with that unwearied, reedy cry
That God has laid His fingers on the sky,
That from those fingers glittering summer runs
Upon the dancer by the dreamless wave.
Why should those lovers that no lovers miss
Dream, until God burn Nature with a kiss?
The man has found no comfort in the grave.

The Lamentation of the Old Pensioner

Although I shelter from the rain
Under a broken tree
My chair was nearest to the fire
In every company
That talked of love or politics,
Ere Time transfigured me.

Though lads are making pikes again
For some conspiracy,
And crazy rascals rage their fill
At human tyranny;
My contemplations are of Time
That has transfigured me.

There's not a woman turns her face
Upon a broken tree,
And yet the beauties that I loved
Are in my memory;
I spit into the face of Time
That has transfigured me.

The Ballad of Father Gilligan

The old priest Peter Gilligan
Was weary night and day;
For half his flock were in their beds,
Or under green sods lay.

Once, while he nodded in a chair,
At the moth-hour of the eve,
Another poor man sent for him,
And he began to grieve.

'I have no rest, nor joy, nor peace,
For people die and die';
And after cried he, 'God forgive!
My body spake not I!'

He knelt, and leaning on the chair
He prayed and fell asleep;
And the moth-hour went from the fields,
And stars began to peep.

They slowly into millions grew,
And leaves shook in the wind;
And God covered the world with shade,
And whispered to mankind.

Upon the time of sparrow-chirp
When the moths came once more,
The old priest Peter Gilligan
Stood upright on the floor.

'Mavrone, mavrone! The man has died
While I slept in the chair';
He roused his horse out of its sleep,
And rode with little care.

He rode now as he never rode,
By rocky lane and fen;
The sick man's wife opened the door:
'Father! you come again!'

'And is the poor man dead?' he cried
'He died an hour ago.'
The old priest Peter Gilligan
In grief swayed to and fro.

'When you were gone, he turned and died
As merry as a bird.'
The old priest Peter Gilligan
He knelt him at that word.

'He Who hath made the night of stars
For souls who tire and bleed,
Sent one of His great angels down
To help me in my need.

'He Who is wrapped in purple robes,
With planets in His care
Had pity on the least of things
Asleep upon a chair.'

The Two Trees

Beloved, gaze in thine own heart,
The holy tree is growing there;
From joy the holy branches start,
And all the trembling flowers they bear.
The changing colours of its fruit
Have dowered the stars with merry light;
The surety of its hidden root
Has planted quiet in the night;
The shaking of its leafy head
Has given the waves their melody,
And made my lips and music wed,
Murmuring a wizard song for thee.
There the Loves a circle go,
The flaming circle of our days,
Gyring, spiring to and fro
In those great ignorant leafy ways;
Remembering all that shaken hair
And how the wingèd sandals dart,
Thine eyes grow full of tender care:
Beloved, gaze in thine own heart.

Gaze no more in the bitter glass
The demons, with their subtle guile,
Lift up before us when they pass,
Or only gaze a little while;
For there a fatal image grows
That the stormy night receives,
Roots half hidden under snows,
Broken boughs and blackened leaves.
For all things turn to barrenness
In the dim glass the demons hold,

The glass of outer weariness,
Made when God slept in times of old.
There, through the broken branches, go
The ravens of unresting thought;
Flying, crying, to and fro,
Cruel claw and hungry throat,
Or else they stand and sniff the wind,
And shake their ragged wings; alas!
Thy tender eyes grow all unkind:
Gaze no more in the bitter glass.

To Some I have Talked with by the Fire

While I wrought out these fitful Danaan rhymes,
My heart would brim with dreams about the times
When we bent down above the fading coals
And talked of the dark folk who live in souls
Of passionate men, like bats in the dead trees;
And of the wayward twilight companies
Who sigh with mingled sorrow and content,
Because their blossoming dreams have never bent
Under the fruit of evil and of good:
And of the embattled flaming multitude
Who rise, wing above wing, flame above flame,
And, like a storm, cry the Ineffable Name,
And with the clashing of their sword-blades make
A rapturous music, till the morning break
And the white hush end all but the loud beat
Of their long wings, the flash of their white feet.

To Ireland in the Coming Times

Know, that I would accounted be
True brother of a company
That sang, to sweeten Ireland's wrong,
Ballad and story, rann and song;
Nor be I any less of them,
Because the red-rose-bordered hem
Of her, whose history began
Before God made the angelic clan,
Trails all about the written page.
When Time began to rant and rage
The measure of her flying feet
Made Ireland's heart begin to beat;
And Time bade all his candles flare
To light a measure here and there;
And may the thoughts of Ireland brood
Upon a measured quietude.

Nor may I less be counted one
With Davis, Mangan, Ferguson,
Because, to him who ponders well,
My rhymes more than their rhyming tell
Of things discovered in the deep,
Where only body's laid asleep.
For the elemental creatures go
About my table to and fro,
That hurry from unmeasured mind
To rant and rage in flood and wind;
Yet he who treads in measured ways
May surely barter gaze for gaze.
Man ever journeys on with them
After the red-rose-bordered hem.

Ah, faeries, dancing under the moon,
A Druid land, a Druid tune!

While still I may, I write for you
The love I lived, the dream I knew.
From our birthday, until we die,
Is but the winking of an eye;
And we, our singing and our love,
What measurer Time has lit above,
And all benighted things that go
About my table to and fro,
Are passing on to where may be,
In truth's consuming ecstasy,
No place for love and dream at all;
For God goes by with white footfall.
I cast my heart into my rhymes,
That you, in the dim coming times,
May know how my heart went with them
After the red-rose-bordered hem.

The Hosting of the Sidhe

The host is riding from Knocknarea
And over the grave of Clooth-na-Bare;
Caoilte tossing his burning hair,
And Niamh calling *Away, come away:*
Empty your heart of its mortal dream.
The winds awaken, the leaves whirl round,
Our cheeks are pale, our hair is unbound,
Our breasts are heaving, our eyes are a-gleam,
Our arms are waving, our lips are apart;
And if any gaze on our rushing band,
We come between him and the deed of his hand,
We come between him and the hope of his heart.
The host is rushing 'twixt night and day,
And where is there hope or deed as fair?
Caoilte tossing his burning hair,
And Niamh calling *Away, come away.*

The Lover tells of the Rose in his Heart

All things uncomely and broken, all things worn out and
   old,
The cry of a child by the roadway, the creak of a
   lumbering cart,
The heavy steps of the ploughman, splashing the wintry
   mould,
Are wronging your image that blossoms a rose in the
   deeps of my heart.

The wrong of unshapely things is a wrong too great to be
   told;
I hunger to build them anew and sit on a green knoll
   apart,
With the earth and the sky and the water, re-made, like a
   casket of gold
For my dreams of your image that blossoms a rose in the
   deeps of my heart.

The Host of the Air

O'Driscoll drove with a song
The wild duck and the drake
From the tall and the tufted reeds
Of the drear Hart Lake.

And he saw how the reeds grew dark
At the coming of night-tide,
And dreamed of the long dim hair
Of Bridget his bride.

He heard while he sang and dreamed
A piper piping away,
And never was piping so sad,
And never was piping so gay.

And he saw young men and young girls
Who danced on a level place,
And Bridget his bride among them,
With a sad and a gay face.

The dancers crowded about him
And many a sweet thing said,
And a young man brought him red wine
And a young girl white bread.

But Bridget drew him by the sleeve
Away from the merry bands,
To old men playing at cards
With a twinkling of ancient hands.

The bread and the wine had a doom,
For these were the host of the air;
He sat and played in a dream
Of her long dim hair.

He played with the merry old men
And thought not of evil chance,
Until one bore Bridget his bride
Away from the merry dance.

He bore her away in his arms,
The handsomest young man there,
And his neck and his breast and his arms
Were drowned in her long dim hair.

O'Driscoll scattered the cards
And out of his dream awoke:
Old men and young men and young girls
Were gone like a drifting smoke;

But he heard high up in the air
A piper piping away,
And never was piping so sad,
And never was piping so gay.

Into the Twilight

Out-worn heart, in a time out-worn,
Come clear of the nets of wrong and right;
Laugh, heart, again in the grey twilight,
Sigh, heart, again in the dew of the morn.

Your mother Eire is always young,
Dew ever shining and twilight grey;
Though hope fall from you and love decay,
Burning in fires of a slanderous tongue.

Come, heart, where hill is heaped upon hill:
For there the mystical brotherhood
Of sun and moon and hollow and wood
And river and stream work out their will;

And God stands winding His lonely horn,
And time and the world are ever in flight;
And love is less kind than the grey twilight,
And hope is less dear than the dew of the morn.

The Song of Wandering Aengus

I went out to the hazel wood,
Because a fire was in my head,
And cut and peeled a hazel wand,
And hooked a berry to a thread;
And when white moths were on the wing,
And moth-like stars were flickering out,
I dropped the berry in a stream
And caught a little silver trout.

When I had laid it on the floor
I went to blow the fire a-flame,
But something rustled on the floor,
And someone called me by my name:
It had become a glimmering girl
With apple blossom in her hair
Who called me by my name and ran
And faded through the brightening air.

Though I am old with wandering
Through hollow lands and hilly lands,
I will find out where she has gone,
And kiss her lips and take her hands;
And walk among long dappled grass,
And pluck till time and times are done
The silver apples of the moon,
The golden apples of the sun.

The Song of the Old Mother

I rise in the dawn, and I kneel and blow
Till the seed of the fire flicker and glow;
And then I must scrub and bake and sweep
Till stars are beginning to blink and peep;
And the young lie long and dream in their bed
Of the matching of ribbons for bosom and head,
And their day goes over in idleness,
And they sigh if the wind but lift a tress:
While I must work because I am old,
And the seed of the fire gets feeble and cold.

The Fiddler of Dooney

When I play on my fiddle in Dooney,
Folk dance like a wave of the sea;
My cousin is priest in Kilvarnet,
My brother in Moharabuiee.

I passed my brother and cousin:
They read in their books of prayer;
I read in my book of songs
I bought at the Sligo fair.

When we come at the end of time,
To Peter sitting in state,
He will smile on the three old spirits,
But call me first through the gate;

For the good are always the merry,
Save by an evil chance,
And the merry love the fiddle,
And the merry love to dance:

And when the folk there spy me,
They will all come up to me,
With 'Here is the fiddler of Dooney!'
And dance like a wave of the sea.

The Heart of the Woman

O what to me the little room
That was brimmed up with prayer and rest;
He bade me out into the gloom,
And my breast lies upon his breast.

O what to me my mother's care,
The house where I was safe and warm;
The shadowy blossom of my hair
Will hide us from the bitter storm.

O hiding hair and dewy eyes,
I am no more with life and death,
My heart upon his warm heart lies,
My breath is mixed into his breath.

He bids his Beloved be at Peace

I hear the Shadowy Horses, their long manes a-shake,
Their hoofs heavy with tumult, their eyes glimmering
  white;
The North unfolds above them clinging, creeping night,
The East her hidden joy before the morning break,
The West weeps in pale dew and sighs passing away,
The South is pouring down roses of crimson fire:
O vanity of Sleep, Hope, Dream, endless Desire,
The Horses of Disaster plunge in the heavy clay:
Beloved, let your eyes half close, and your heart beat
Over my heart, and your hair fall over my breast,
Drowning love's lonely hour in deep twilight of rest,
And hiding their tossing manes and their tumultuous feet.

A Poet to his Beloved

I bring you with reverent hands
The books of my numberless dreams,
White woman that passion has worn
As the tide wears the dove-grey sands,
And with heart more old than the horn
That is brimmed from the pale fire of time:
White woman with numberless dreams,
I bring you my passionate rhyme.

To his Heart, bidding it have no Fear

Be you still, be you still, trembling heart;
Remember the wisdom out of the old days:
Him who trembles before the flame and the flood,
And the winds that blow through the starry ways,
Let the starry winds and the flame and the flood
Cover over and hide, for he has no part
With the proud, majestical multitude.

The Lover asks Forgiveness because of his Many Moods

If this importunate heart trouble your peace
With words lighter than air,
Or hopes that in mere hoping flicker and cease;
Crumple the rose in your hair;
And cover your lips with odorous twilight and say,
'O Hearts of wind-blown flame!
O Winds, elder than changing of night and day,
That murmuring and longing came,
From marble cities loud with tabors of old
In dove-grey faery lands;
From battle-banners, fold upon purple fold,
Queens wrought with glimmering hands;
That saw young Niamh hover with love-lorn face
Above the wandering tide;
And lingered in the hidden desolate place
Where the last Phoenix died
And wrapped the flames above his holy head;
And still murmur and long:
O Piteous Hearts, changing till change be dead
In a tumultuous song':
And cover the pale blossoms of your breast
With your dim heavy hair,
And trouble with a sigh for all things longing for rest
The odorous twilight there.

He tells of a Valley full of Lovers

I dreamed that I stood in a valley, and amid sighs,
For happy lovers passed two by two where I stood;
And I dreamed my lost love came stealthily out of the
    wood
With her cloud-pale eyelids falling on dream-dimmed
    eyes:
I cried in my dream, O women, bid the young men lay
Their heads on your knees, and drown their eyes with your hair,
Or remembering hers they will find no other face fair
Till all the valleys of the world have been withered away.

He tells of the Perfect Beauty

O cloud-pale eyelids, dream-dimmed eyes,
The poets labouring all their days
To build a perfect beauty in rhyme
Are overthrown by a woman's gaze
And by the unlabouring brood of the skies:
And therefore my heart will bow, when dew
Is dropping sleep, until God burn time,
Before the unlabouring stars and you.

The Blessed

Cumhal called out, bending his head,
Till Dathi came and stood,
With a blink in his eyes at the cave-mouth,
Between the wind and the wood.

And Cumhal said, bending his knees,
'I have come by the windy way
To gather the half of your blessedness
And learn to pray when you pray.

'I can bring you salmon out of the streams
And heron out of the skies.'
But Dathi folded his hands and smiled
With the secrets of God in his eyes.

And Cumhal saw like a drifting smoke
All manner of blessed souls,
Women and children, young men with books,
And old men with croziers and stoles.

'Praise God and God's mother,' Dathi said,
'For God and God's mother have sent
The blessedest souls that walk in the world
To fill your heart with content.'

'And which is the blessedest,' Cumhal said,
'Where all are comely and good?
Is it these that with golden thuribles
Are singing about the wood?'

'My eyes are blinking,' Dathi said,
'With the secrets of God half blind,
But I can see where the wind goes
And follow the way of the wind;

'And blessedness goes where the wind goes,
And when it is gone we are dead;
I see the blessedest soul in the world
And he nods a drunken head.

'O blessedness comes in the night and the day
And whither the wise heart knows;
And one has seen in the redness of wine
The Incorruptible Rose,

'That drowsily drops faint leaves on him
And the sweetness of desire,
While time and the world are ebbing away
In twilights of dew and of fire.'

He wishes for the Cloths of Heaven

Had I the heavens' embroidered cloths,
Enwrought with golden and silver light,
The blue and the dim and the dark cloths
Of night and light and the half light,
I would spread the cloths under your feet:
But I, being poor, have only my dreams;
I have spread my dreams under your feet;
Tread softly because you tread on my dreams.

The Travail of Passion

When the flaming lute-thronged angelic door is wide;
When an immortal passion breathes in mortal clay;
Our hearts endure the scourge, the plaited thorns, the way
Crowded with bitter faces, the wounds in palm and side,
The vinegar-heavy sponge, the flowers by Kedron stream:
We will bend down and loosen our hair over you,
That it may drop faint perfume, and be heavy with dew,
Lilies of death-pale hope, roses of passionate dream.

In the Seven Woods

I have heard the pigeons of the Seven Woods
Make their faint thunder, and the garden bees
Hum in the lime-tree flowers; and put away
The unavailing outcries and the old bitterness
That empty the heart. I have forgot awhile
Tara uprooted, and new commonness
Upon the throne and crying about the streets
And hanging its paper flowers from post to post,
Because it is alone of all things happy.
I am contented for I know that Quiet
Wanders laughing and eating her wild heart
Among pigeons and bees, while that Great Archer,
Who but awaits His hour to shoot, still hangs
A cloudy quiver over Parc-na-Lee.

The Old Age of Queen Maeve

A certain poet in outlandish clothes
Gathered a crowd in some Byzantine lane,
Talked of his country and its people, sang
To some stringed instrument none there had seen,
A wall behind his back, over his head
A latticed window. His glance went up at times
As though one listened there, and his voice sank
Or let its meaning mix into the strings.

Maeve the great queen was pacing to and fro,
Between the walls covered with beaten bronze,
In her high house at Cruachan; the long hearth,
Flickering with ash and hazel, but half showed
Where the tired horse-boys lay upon the rushes,
Or on the benches underneath the walls,
In comfortable sleep; all living slept
But that great queen, who more than half the night
Had paced from door to fire and fire to door.
Though now in her old age, in her young age
She had been beautiful in that old way
That's all but gone; for the proud heart is gone
And the fool heart of the counting-house fears all
But soft beauty and indolent desire.
She could have called over the rim of the world
Whatever woman's lover had hit her fancy,
And yet had been great-bodied and great-limbed,
Fashioned to be the mother of strong children;
And she'd had lucky eyes and a high heart,
And wisdom that caught fire like the dried flax,
At need, and made her beautiful and fierce,
Sudden and laughing.

O unquiet heart,
Why do you praise another, praising her,
As if there were no tale but your own tale
Worth knitting to a measure of sweet sound?
Have I not bid you tell of that great queen
Who has been buried some two thousand years?

When night was at its deepest, a wild goose
Cried from the porter's lodge, and with long clamour
Shook the ale-horns and shields upon their hooks;
But the horse-boys slept on, as though some power
Had filled the house with Druid heaviness;
And wondering who of the many-changing Sidhe
Had come as in the old times to counsel her,
Maeve walked, yet with slow footfall being old,
To that small chamber by the outer gate.
The porter slept, although he sat upright
With still and stony limbs and open eyes.
Maeve waited, and when that ear-piercing noise
Broke from his parted lips and broke again,
She laid a hand on either of his shoulders,
And shook him wide awake, and bid him say
Who of the wandering many-changing ones
Had troubled his sleep. But all he had to say
Was that, the air being heavy and the dogs
More still than they had been for a good month,
He had fallen asleep, and, though he had dreamed
    nothing,
He could remember when he had had fine dreams.
It was before the time of the great war
Over the White-Horned Bull and the Brown Bull.

She turned away; he turned again to sleep

That no god troubled now, and, wondering
What matters were afoot among the Sidhe,
Maeve walked through that great hall, and with a sigh
Lifted the curtain of her sleeping-room,
Remembering that she too had seemed divine
To many thousand eyes, and to her own
One that the generations had long waited
That work too difficult for mortal hands
Might be accomplished. Bunching the curtain up
She saw her husband Ailell sleeping there,
And thought of days when he'd had a straight body,
And of that famous Fergus, Nessa's husband,
Who had been the lover of her middle life.

Suddenly Ailell spoke out of his sleep,
And not with his own voice or a man's voice,
But with the burning, live, unshaken voice
Of those that, it may be, can never age.
He said, 'High Queen of Cruachan and Mag Ai,
A king of the Great Plain would speak with you.'
And with glad voice Maeve answered him, 'What king
Of the far-wandering shadows has come to me
As in the old days when they would come and go
About my threshold to counsel and to help?'
The parted lips replied, 'I seek your help,
For I am Aengus and I am crossed in love.'
'How may a mortal whose life gutters out
Help them that wander with hand clasping hand,
Their haughty images that cannot wither,
For all the beauty's like a hollow dream,
Mirrored in streams that neither hail nor rain
Nor the cold North has troubled?'
                              He replied,

'I am from those rivers and I bid you call
The children of the Maines out of sleep,
And set them digging under Bual's hill.
We shadows, while they uproot his earthy house,
Will overthrow his shadows and carry off
Caer, his blue-eyed daughter that I love.
I helped your fathers when they built these walls,
And I would have your help in my great need,
Queen of high Cruachan'.

                       'I obey your will
With speedy feet and a most thankful heart:
For you have been, O Aengus of the birds,
Our giver of good counsel and good luck.'
And with a groan, as if the mortal breath
Could but awaken sadly upon lips
That happier breath had moved, her husband turned
Face downward, tossing in a troubled sleep;
But Maeve, and not with a slow feeble foot,
Came to the threshold of the painted house
Where her grandchildren slept, and cried aloud,
Until the pillared dark began to stir
With shouting and the clang of unhooked arms.
She told them of the many-changing ones;
And all that night, and all through the next day
To middle night, they dug into the hill.
At middle night great cats with silver claws,
Bodies of shadow and blind eyes like pearls,
Came up out of the hole, and red-eared hounds
With long white bodies came out of the air
Suddenly, and ran at them and harried them.

The Maines' children dropped their spades, and stood
With quaking joints and terror-strucken faces,

Till Maeve called out, 'These are but common men.
The Maines' children have not dropped their spades
Because Earth, crazy for its broken power,
Casts up a show and the winds answer it
With holy shadows.' Her high heart was glad,
And when the uproar ran along the grass
She followed with light footfall in the midst,
Till it died out where an old thorn-tree stood.

Friend of these many years, you too had stood
With equal courage in that whirling rout;
For you, although you've not her wandering heart,
Have all that greatness, and not her's alone,
For there is no high story about queens
In any ancient book but tells of you;
And when I've heard how they grew old and died,
Or fell into unhappiness I've said;
'She will grow old and die and she has wept!'
And when I'd write it out anew, the words,
Half crazy with the thought, She too has wept!
Outrun the measure.
                              I'd tell of that great queen
Who stood amid a silence by the thorn
Until two lovers came out of the air
With bodies made out of soft fire. The one,
About whose face birds wagged their fiery wings,
Said, 'Aengus and his sweetheart give their thanks
To Maeve and to Maeve's household, owing all
In owing them the bride-bed that gives peace.'
Then Maeve: 'O Aengus, Master of all lovers,
A thousand years ago you held high talk
With the first kings of many pillared Cruachan.
O when will you grow weary?'

They had vanished;
But out of the dark air over her head there came
A murmur of soft words and meeting lips.

Baile and Aillinn

ARGUMENT. *Baile and Aillinn were lovers, but Aengus, the Master of Love, wishing them to be happy in his own land among the dead, told to each a story of the other's death, so that their hearts were broken and they died.*

I hardly hear the curlew cry,
Nor the grey rush when wind is high,
Before my thoughts begin to run
On the heir of Ulad, Buan's son,
Baile, who had the honey mouth;
And that mild woman of the south,
Aillinn, who was King Lugaid's heir.
Their love was never drowned in care
Of this or that thing, nor grew cold
Because their bodies had grown old.
Being forbid to marry on earth,
They blossomed to immortal mirth.

About the time when Christ was born,
When the long wars for the White Horn
And the Brown Bull had not yet come,
Young Baile Honey-Mouth, whom some
Called rather Baile Little-Land,
Rode out of Emain with a band
Of harpers and young men, and they
Imagined, as they struck the way
To many-pastured Muirthemne,
That all things fell out happily,
And there, for all that fools had said,
Baile and Aillinn would be wed.

They found an old man running there,

He had ragged long grass-coloured hair;
He had knees that stuck out of his hose;
He had puddle-water in his shoes;
He had half a cloak to keep him dry,
Although he had a squirrel's eye.

O wandering birds and rushy beds,
You put such folly in our heads
With all this crying in the wind,
No common love is to our mind,
And our poor Kate or Nan is less
Than any whose unhappiness
Awoke the harp-strings long ago.
Yet they that know all things but know
That all this life can give us is
A child's laughter, a woman's kiss.
Who was it put so great a scorn
In the grey reeds that night and morn
Are trodden and broken by the herds,
And in the light bodies of birds
That north wind tumbles to and fro
And pinches among hail and snow?

That runner said: 'I am from the south;
I run to Baile Honey-Mouth
To tell him how the girl Aillinn
Rode from the country of her kin,
And old and young men rode with her:
For all that country had been astir
If anybody half as fair
Had chosen a husband anywhere
But where it could see her every day.
When they had ridden a little way

An old man caught the horse's head
With: 'You must home again, and wed
With somebody in your own land.'
A young man cried and kissed her hand,
'O lady, wed with one of us;'
And when no face grew piteous
For any gentle thing she spake,
She fell and died of the heart-break'.

Because a lover's heart's worn out,
Being tumbled and blown about
By its own blind imagining,
And will believe that anything
That is bad enough to be true, is true,
Baile's heart was broken in two;
And he, being laid upon green boughs,
Was carried to the goodly house
Where the Hound of Ulad sat before
The brazen pillars of his door,
His face bowed low to weep the end
Of the harper's daughter and her friend.
For although years had passed away
He always wept them on that day,
For on that day they had been betrayed;
And now that Honey-Mouth is laid
Under a cairn of sleepy stone
Before his eyes, he has tears for none,
Although he is carrying stone, but two
For whom the cairn's but heaped anew.

We hold, because our memory is
So full of that thing and of this
That out of sight is out of mind.

But the grey rush under the wind
And the grey bird with crooked bill
Have such long memories that they still
Remember Deirdre and her man;
And when we walk with Kate or Nan
About the windy water-side,
Our heart can hear the voices chide.
How could we be so soon content,
Who know the way that Naoise went?
And they have news of Deirdre's eyes,
Who being lovely was so wise —
Ah wise, my heart knows well how wise.

Now had that old gaunt crafty one,
Gathering his cloak about him, run
Where Aillinn rode with waiting maids,
Who amid leafy lights and shades
Dreamed of the hands that would unlace
Their bodices in some dim place
When they had come to the marriage-bed;
And harpers, pacing with high head
As though their music were enough
To make the savage heart of love
Grow gentle without sorrowing,
Imagining and pondering
Heaven knows what calamity;

'Another's hurried off,' cried he,
'From heat and cold and wind and wave;
They have heaped the stones above his grave
In Muirthemne, and over it
In changeless Ogham letters writ —
Baile that was of Rury's seed.

But the gods long ago decreed
No waiting-maid should ever spread
Baile and Aillinn's marriage-bed,
For they should clip and clip again
Where wild bees hive on the Great Plain.
Therefore it is but little news
That put this hurry in my shoes.'

Then seeing that he scarce had spoke
Before her love-worn heart had broke,
He ran and laughed until he came
To that high hill the herdsmen name
The Hill Seat of Leighin, because
Some god or king had made the laws
That held the land together there,
In old times among the clouds of the air.

That old man climbed; the day grew dim;
Two swans came flying up to him,
Linked by a gold chain each to each,
And with low murmuring laughing speech
Alighted on the windy grass.
They knew him: his changed body was
Tall, proud and ruddy, and light wings
Were hovering over the harp-strings
That Edain, Midhir's wife, had wove
In the hid place, being crazed by love.

What shall I call them? fish that swim,
Scale rubbing scale where light is dim
By a broad water-lily leaf;
Or mice in the one wheaten sheaf
Forgotten at the threshing place;

Or birds lost in the one clear space
Of morning light in a dim sky;
Or, it may be, the eyelids of one eye,
Or the door-pillars of one house,
Or two sweet blossoming apple-boughs
That have one shadow on the ground;
Or the two strings that made one sound
Where that wise harper's finger ran.
For this young girl and this young man
Have happiness without an end,
Because they have made so good a friend.

They know all wonders, for they pass
The towery gates of Gorias,
And Findrias and Falias,
And long-forgotten Murias,
Among the giant kings whose hoard,
Cauldron and spear and stone and sword,
Was robbed before earth gave the wheat;
Wandering from broken street to street
They come where some huge watcher is,
And tremble with their love and kiss.

They know undying things, for they
Wander where earth withers away,
Though nothing troubles the great streams
But light from the pale stars, and gleams
From the holy orchards, where there is none
But fruit that is of precious stone,
Or apples of the sun and moon.

What were our praise to them? They eat
Quiet's wild heart, like daily meat;

Who when night thickens are afloat
On dappled skins in a glass boat,
Far out under a windless sky;
While over them birds of Aengus fly,
And over the tiller and the prow,
And waving white wings to and fro
Awaken wanderings of light air
To stir their coverlet and their hair.

And poets found, old writers say,
A yew-tree where his body lay;
But a wild apple hid the grass
With its sweet blossom where hers was;
And being in good heart, because
A better time had come again
After the deaths of many men,
And that long fighting at the ford,
They wrote on tablets of thin board,
Made of the apple and the yew,
All the love stories that they knew.

Let rush and bird cry out their fill
Of the harper's daughter if they will,
Beloved, I am not afraid of her
She is not wiser nor lovelier,
And you are more high of heart than she,
For all her wanderings over-sea;
But I'd have bird and rush forget
Those other two; for never yet
Has lover lived but longed to wive
Like them that are no more alive.

The Arrow

I thought of your beauty and this arrow,
Made out of a wild thought, is in my marrow.
There's no man may look upon her, no man,
As when newly grown to be a woman,
Tall and noble but with face and bosom
Delicate in colour as apple blossom.
This beauty's kinder, yet for a reason
I could weep that the old is out of season.

Adam's Curse

We sat together at one summer's end,
That beautiful mild woman your close friend,
And you and I, and talked of poetry.
I said: 'A line will take us hours maybe;
Yet if it does not seem a moment's thought,
Our stitching and unstitching has been naught.
Better go down upon your marrow-bones
And scrub a kitchen pavement, or break stones
Like an old pauper, in all kinds of weather;
For to articulate sweet sounds together
Is to work harder than all these, and yet
Be thought an idler by the noisy set
Of bankers, schoolmasters, and clergymen
The martyrs call the world.'

                    And thereupon
That beautiful mild woman for whose sake
There's many a one shall find out all heartache
On finding that her voice is sweet and low
Replied: 'To be born woman is to know —
Although they do not talk of it at school —
That we must labour to be beautiful.'

I said, 'It's certain there is no fine thing
Since Adam's fall but needs much labouring.
There have been lovers who thought love should be
So much compounded of high courtesy
That they would sigh and quote with learned looks
Precedents out of beautiful old books;
Yet now it seems an idle trade enough'.

We sat grown quiet at the name of love;
We saw the last embers of daylight die,
And in the trembling blue-green of the sky
A moon, worn as if it had been a shell
Washed by time's waters as they rose and fell
About the stars and broke in days and years.

I had a thought for no one's but your ears:
That you were beautiful, and that I strove
To love you in the old high way of love;
That it had all seemed happy, and yet we'd grown
As weary-hearted as that hollow moon.

Red Hanrahan's Song about Ireland

The old brown thorn-trees break in two high over
    Cummen Strand,
Under a bitter black wind that blows from the left hand;
Our courage breaks like an old tree in a black wind and
    dies,
But we have hidden in our hearts the flame out of the
    eyes
Of Cathleen, the daughter of Houlihan.

The wind has bundled up the clouds high over
    Knocknarea,
And thrown the thunder on the stones for all that Maeve
    can say.
Angers that are like noisy clouds have set our hearts abeat;
But we have all bent low and low and kissed the quiet
    feet
Of Cathleen, the daughter of Houlihan.

The yellow pool has overflowed high up on Clooth-na-
    Bare,
For the wet winds are blowing out of the clinging air;
Like heavy flooded waters our bodies and our blood;
But purer than a tall candle before the Holy Rood
Is Cathleen, the daughter of Houlihan.

Under the Moon

I have no happiness in dreaming of Brycelinde,
Nor Avalon the grass-green hollow, nor Joyous Isle,
Where one found Lancelot crazed and hid him for
    a while;
Nor Ulad, when Naoise had thrown a sail upon the wind;
Nor lands that seem too dim to be burdens on the heart:
Land-under-Wave, where out of the moon's light and
    the sun's
Seven old sisters wind the threads of the long lived ones,
Land-of-the-Tower, where Aengus has thrown the gates
    apart,
And Wood-of-Wonders, where one kills an ox at dawn,
To find it when night falls laid on a golden bier.
Therein are many queens like Branwen, and Guinivere;
And Niamh and Laban and Fand, who could change to
    an otter or fawn,
And the wood-woman, whose lover was changed to
    a blue-eyed hawk;
And whether I go in my dreams by woodland, or dun, or
    shore,
Or on the unpeopled waves with kings to pull at the oar,
I hear the harp-string praise them, or hear their mournful
    talk.

Because of something told under the famished horn
Of the hunter's moon, that hung between the night and
    the day,
To dream of women whose beauty was folded in dismay,
Even in an old story, is a burden not to be borne.

The Old Men Admiring Themselves in the Water

I heard the old, old men say,
'Everything alters,
And one by one we drop away.'
They had hands like claws, and their knees
Were twisted like the old thorn-trees
By the waters.
I heard the old, old men say,
'All that's beautiful drifts away
Like the waters.'

O Do Not Love Too Long

Sweetheart, do not love too long:
I loved long and long,
And grew to be out of fashion
Like an old song.

All through the years of our youth
Neither could have known
Their own thought from the other's,
We were so much at one.

But O, in a minute she changed –
O do not love too long,
Or you will grow out of fashion
Like an old song.

Never Give all the Heart

Never give all the heart, for love
Will hardly seem worth thinking of
To passionate women if it seem
Certain, and they never dream
That it fades out from kiss to kiss;
For everything that's lovely is
But a brief, dreamy, kind delight.
O never give the heart outright,
For they, for all smooth lips can say,
Have given their hearts up to the play.
And who could play it well enough
If deaf and dumb and blind with love?
He that made this knows all the cost,
For he gave all his heart and lost.

A Woman Homer Sung

If any man drew near
When I was young,
I thought, 'He holds her dear,'
And shook with hate and fear.
But oh! 'twas bitter wrong
If he could pass her by
With an indifferent eye.

Whereon I wrote and wrought,
And now, being grey,
I dream that I have brought
To such a pitch my thought
That coming time can say,
'He shadowed in a glass
What thing her body was.'

For she had fiery blood
When I was young,
And trod so sweetly proud
As 'twere upon a cloud,
A woman Homer sung,
That life and letters seem
But an heroic dream.

Words

I had this thought a while ago,
'My darling cannot understand
What I have done, or what would do
In this blind bitter land.'

And I grew weary of the sun
Until my thoughts cleared up again,
Remembering that the best I have done
Was done to make it plain;

That every year I have cried, 'At length
My darling understands it all,
Because I have come into my strength,
And words obey my call';

That had she done so who can say
What would have shaken from the sieve?
I might have thrown poor words away
And been content to live.

No Second Troy

Why should I blame her that she filled my days
With misery, or that she would of late
Have taught to ignorant men most violent ways,
Or hurled the little streets upon the great,
Had they but courage equal to desire?
What could have made her peaceful with a mind
That nobleness made simple as a fire,
With beauty like a tightened bow, a kind
That is not natural in an age like this,
Being high and solitary and most stern?
Why, what could she have done, being what she is?
Was there another Troy for her to burn?

Reconciliation

Some may have blamed you that you took away
The verses that could move them on the day
When, the ears being deafened, the sight of the eyes blind
With lightning, you went from me, and I could find
Nothing to make a song about but kings,
Helmets, and swords, and half-forgotten things
That were like memories of you — but now
We'll out, for the world lives as long ago;
And while we're in our laughing, weeping fit,
Hurl helmets, crowns, and swords into the pit.
But, dear, cling close to me; since you were gone,
My barren thoughts have chilled me to the bone.

King and No King

'Would it were anything but merely voice!'
The No King cried who after that was King,
Because he had not heard of anything
That balanced with a word is more than noise;
Yet Old Romance being kind, let him prevail
Somewhere or somehow that I have forgot,
Though he'd but cannon — Whereas we that had thought
To have lit upon as clean and sweet a tale
Have been defeated by that pledge you gave
In momentary anger long ago;
And I that have not your faith, how shall I know
That in the blinding light beyond the grave
We'll find so good a thing as that we have lost?
The hourly kindness, the day's common speech,
The habitual content of each with each
When neither soul nor body has been crossed.

Peace

Ah, that Time could touch a form
That could show what Homer's age
Bred to be a hero's wage.
'Were not all her life but storm,
Would not painters paint a form
Of such noble lines,' I said,
'Such a delicate high head,
All that sternness amid charm,
All that sweetness amid strength?'
Ah, but peace that comes at length,
Came when Time had touched her form.

Against Unworthy Praise

O heart, be at peace, because
Nor knave nor dolt can break
What's not for their applause,
Being for a woman's sake.
Enough if the work has seemed,
So did she your strength renew,
A dream that a lion had dreamed
Till the wilderness cried aloud,
A secret between you two,
Between the proud and the proud.

What, still you would have their praise!
But here's a haughtier text,
The labyrinth of her days
That her own strangeness perplexed;
And how what her dreaming gave
Earned slander, ingratitude,
From self-same dolt and knave;
Aye, and worse wrong than these,
Yet she, singing upon her road,
Half lion, half child, is at peace.

The Fascination of What's Difficult

The fascination of what's difficult
Has dried the sap out of my veins, and rent
Spontaneous joy and natural content
Out of my heart. There's something ails our colt
That must, as if it had not holy blood
Nor on Olympus leaped from cloud to cloud,
Shiver under the lash, strain, sweat and jolt
As though it dragged road metal. My curse on plays
That have to be set up in fifty ways,
On the day's war with every knave and dolt,
Theatre business, management of men.
I swear before the dawn comes round again
I'll find the stable and pull out the bolt.

A Drinking Song

Wine comes in at the mouth
And love comes in at the eye;
That's all we shall know for truth
Before we grow old and die.
I lift the glass to my mouth,
I look at you, and I sigh.

The Coming of Wisdom with Time

Though leaves are many, the root is one;
Through all the lying days of my youth
I swayed my leaves and flowers in the sun;
Now I may wither into the truth.

The Mask

'Put off that mask of burning gold
With emerald eyes.'
'O no, my dear, you make so bold
To find if hearts be wild and wise,
And yet not cold.'

'I would but find what's there to find,
Love or deceit.'
'It was the mask engaged your mind,
And after set your heart to beat,
Not what's behind.'

'But lest you are my enemy,
I must enquire.'
'O no, my dear, let all that be;
What matter, so there is but fire
In you, in me?'

Upon a House shaken by the Land Agitation

How should the world be luckier if this house,
Where passion and precision have been one
Time out of mind, became too ruinous
To breed the lidless eye that loves the sun?
And the sweet laughing eagle thoughts that grow
Where wings have memory of wings, and all
That comes of the best knit to the best? Although
Mean roof-trees were the sturdier for its fall,
How should their luck run high enough to reach
The gifts that govern men, and after these
To gradual Time's last gift, a written speech
Wrought of high laughter, loveliness and ease?

At the Abbey Theatre

Dear Craoibhin Aoibhin, look into our case.
When we are high and airy hundreds say
That if we hold that flight they'll leave the place,
While those same hundreds mock another day
Because we have made our art of common things,
So bitterly, you'd dream they longed to look
All their lives through into some drift of wings.
You've dandled them and fed them from the book
And know them to the bone; impart to us —
We'll keep the secret — a new trick to please.
Is there a bridle for this Proteus
That turns and changes like his draughty seas?
Or is there none, most popular of men,
But when they mock us, that we mock again?

These are the Clouds

These are the clouds about the fallen sun,
The majesty that shuts his burning eye:
The weak lay hand on what the strong has done,
Till that be tumbled that was lifted high
And discord follow upon unison,
And all things at one common level lie.
And therefore, friend, if your great race were run
And these things came, so much the more thereby
Have you made greatness your companion,
Although it be for children that you sigh:
These are the clouds about the fallen sun,
The majesty that shuts his burning eye.

At Galway Races

There where the course is,
Delight makes all of the one mind,
The riders upon the galloping horses,
The crowd that closes in behind:
We, too, had good attendance once,
Hearers and hearteners of the work;
Aye, horsemen for companions,
Before the merchant and the clerk
Breathed on the world with timid breath.
Sing on: somewhere at some new moon,
We'll learn that sleeping is not death,
Hearing the whole earth change its tune,
Its flesh being wild, and it again
Crying aloud as the racecourse is,
And we find hearteners among men
That ride upon horses.

All Things can Tempt me

All things can tempt me from this craft of verse:
One time it was a woman's face, or worse —
The seeming needs of my fool-driven land;
Now nothing but comes readier to the hand
Than this accustomed toil. When I was young,
I had not given a penny for a song
Did not the poet sing it with such airs
That one believed he had a sword upstairs;
Yet would be now, could I but have my wish,
Colder and dumber and deafer than a fish.

Brown Penny

I whispered, 'I am too young,'
And then, 'I am old enough';
Wherefore I threw a penny
To find out if I might love.
'Go and love, go and love, young man,
If the lady be young and fair.'
Ah, penny, brown penny, brown penny,
I am looped in the loops of her hair.

O, love is the crooked thing,
There is nobody wise enough
To find out all that is in it,
For he would be thinking of love
Till the stars had run away,
And the shadows eaten the moon.
Ah, penny, brown penny, brown penny,
One cannot begin it too soon.

The Grey Rock

Poets with whom I learned my trade,
Companions of the Cheshire Cheese,
Here's an old story I've re-made,
Imagining 'twould better please
Your ears than stories now in fashion,
Though you may think I waste my breath
Pretending that there can be passion
That has more life in it than death,
And though at bottling of your wine
Old wholesome Goban had no say;
The moral's yours because it's mine.

When cups went round at close of day —
Is not that how good stories run? —
The gods were sitting at the board
In their great house at Slievenamon.
They sang a drowsy song, or snored,
For all were full of wine and meat.
The smoky torches made a glare
On metal Goban 'd hammered at,
On old deep silver rolling there
Or on some still unemptied cup
That he, when frenzy stirred his thews,
Had hammered out on mountain top
To hold the sacred stuff he brews
That only gods may buy of him.

Now from that juice that made them wise
All those had lifted up the dim
Imaginations of their eyes,
For one that was like woman made

Before their sleepy eyelids ran
And trembling with her passion said,
'Come out and dig for a dead man,
Who's burrowing somewhere in the ground,
And mock him to his face and then
Hollo him on with horse and hound,
For he is the worst of all dead men.'

We should be dazed and terror-struck,
If we but saw in dreams that room,
Those wine-drenched eyes, and curse our luck
That emptied all our days to come.
I knew a woman none could please,
Because she dreamed when but a child
Of men and women made like these;
And after, when her blood ran wild,
Had ravelled her own story out,
And said, 'In two or in three years
I need must marry some poor lout,'
And having said it burst in tears.

Since, tavern comrades, you have died,
Maybe your images have stood,
Mere bone and muscle thrown aside,
Before that roomful or as good.
You had to face your ends when young —
'Twas wine or women, or some curse —
But never made a poorer song
That you might have a heavier purse,
Nor gave loud service to a cause
That you might have a troop of friends.
You kept the Muses' sterner laws,
And unrelenting faced your ends,

And therefore earned the right — and yet
Dowson and Johnson most I praise —
To troop with those the world's forgot,
And copy their proud steady gaze.

'The Danish troop was driven out
Between the dawn and dusk' she said;
'Although the event was long in doubt,
Although the King of Ireland's dead
And half the kings, before sundown
All was accomplished.'
              'When this day
Murrough, the King of Ireland's son,
Foot after foot was giving way,
He and his best troops back to back
Had perished there, but the Danes ran,
Stricken with panic from the attack,
The shouting of an unseen man;
And being thankful Murrough found,
Led by a footsole dipped in blood
That had made prints upon the ground,
Where by old thorn-trees that man stood;
And though when he gazed here and there,
He had but gazed on thorn-trees, spoke,
"Who is the friend that seems but air
And yet could give so fine a stroke?"
Thereon a young man met his eye,
Who said, "Because she held me in
Her love, and would not have me die,
Rock-nurtured Aoife took a pin,
And pushing it into my shirt,
Promised that for a pin's sake,
No man should see to do me hurt;

But there it's gone; I will not take
The fortune that had been my shame
Seeing, King's son, what wounds you have."
'Twas roundly spoke, but when night came
He had betrayed me to his grave,
For he and the King's son were dead.
I'd promised him two hundred years,
And when for all I'd done or said —
And these immortal eyes shed tears —
He claimed his country's need was most,
I'd save his life, yet for the sake
Of a new friend he has turned a ghost.
What does he care if my heart break?
I call for spade and horse and hound
That we may harry him.' Thereon
She cast herself upon the ground
And rent her clothes and made her moan:
'Why are they faithless when their might
Is from the holy shades that rove
The grey rock and the windy light?
Why should the faithfullest heart most love
The bitter sweetness of false faces?
Why must the lasting love what passes,
Why are the gods by men betrayed!'

But thereon every god stood up
With a slow smile and without sound,
And stretching forth his arm and cup
To where she moaned upon the ground,
Suddenly drenched her to the skin;
And she with Goban's wine adrip,
No more remembering what had been,
Stared at the gods with laughing lip.

I have kept my faith, though faith was tried,
To that rock-born, rock-wandering foot,
And the world's altered since you died,
And I am in no good repute
With the loud host before the sea,
That think sword-strokes were better meant
Than lover's music — let that be,
So that the wandering foot's content.

The Two Kings

King Eochaid came at sundown to a wood
Westward of Tara. Hurrying to his queen
He had out-ridden his war-wasted men
That with empounded cattle trod the mire;
And where beech trees had mixed a pale green light
With the ground-ivy's blue, he saw a stag
Whiter than curds, its eyes the tint of the sea.
Because it stood upon his path and seemed
More hands in height than any stag in the world
He sat with tightened rein and loosened mouth
Upon his trembling horse, then drove the spur;
But the stag stooped and ran at him, and passed,
Rending the horse's flank. King Eochaid reeled
Then drew his sword to hold its levelled point
Against the stag. When horn and steel were met
The horn resounded as though it had been silver,
A sweet, miraculous, terrifying sound.
Horn locked in sword, they tugged and struggled there
As though a stag and unicorn were met
Among the African Mountains of the Moon,
Until at last the double horns, drawn backward,
Butted below the single and so pierced
The entrails of the horse. Dropping his sword
King Eochaid seized the horns in his strong hands
And stared into the sea-green eye, and so
Hither and thither to and fro they trod
Till all the place was beaten into mire.
The strong thigh and the agile thigh were met,
The hands that gathered up the might of the world,
And hoof and horn that had sucked in their speed
Amid the elaborate wilderness of the air.

Through bush they plunged and over ivied root,
And where the stone struck fire, while in the leaves
A squirrel whinnied and a bird screamed out;
But when at last he forced those sinewy flanks
Against a beech-bole, he threw down the beast
And knelt above it with drawn knife. On the instant
It vanished like a shadow, and a cry
So mournful that it seemed the cry of one
Who had lost some unimaginable treasure
Wandered between the blue and the green leaf
And climbed into the air, crumbling away,
Till all had seemed a shadow or a vision
But for the trodden mire, the pool of blood,
The disembowelled horse.

           King Eochaid ran,
Toward peopled Tara, nor stood to draw his breath
Until he came before the painted wall,
The posts of polished yew, circled with bronze,
Of the great door; but though the hanging lamps
Showed their faint light through the unshuttered
  windows,
Nor door, nor mouth, nor slipper made a noise,
Nor on the ancient beaten paths, that wound
From well-side or from plough-land, was there noise;
Nor had there been the noise of living thing
Before him or behind, but that far-off
On the horizon edge bellowed the herds.
Knowing that silence brings no good to kings,
And mocks returning victory, he passed
Between the pillars with a beating heart
And saw where in the midst of the great hall
Pale-faced, alone upon a bench, Edain
Sat upright with a sword before her feet.

Her hands on either side had gripped the bench,
Her eyes were cold and steady, her lips tight.
Some passion had made her stone. Hearing a foot
She started and then knew whose foot it was;
But when he thought to take her in his arms
She motioned him afar, and rose and spoke:
'I have sent among the fields or to the woods
The fighting men and servants of this house,
For I would have your judgment upon one
Who is self-accused. If she be innocent
She would not look in any known man's face
Till judgment has been given, and if guilty,
Would never look again on known man's face.'
And at these words he paled, as she had paled,
Knowing that he should find upon her lips
The meaning of that monstrous day.
                                        Then she:
'You brought me where your brother Ardan sat
Always in his one seat, and bid me care him
Through that strange illness that had fixed him there,
And should he die to heap his burial-mound
And carve his name in Ogham.' Eochaid said,
'He lives?' 'He lives and is a healthy man.'
'While I have him and you it matters little
What man you have lost, what evil you have found.'
'I bid them make his bed under this roof
And carried him his food with my own hands,
And so the weeks passed by. But when I said,
"What is this trouble?" he would answer nothing,
Though always at my words his trouble grew;
And I but asked the more, till he cried out,
Weary of many questions: "There are things
That make the heart akin to the dumb stone."

Then I replied: "Although you hide a secret,
Hopeless and dear, or terrible to think on,
Speak it, that I may send through the wide world
For medicine." Thereon he cried aloud,
"Day after day you question me, and I,
Because there is such a storm amid my thoughts
I shall be carried in the gust, command,
Forbid, beseech and waste my breath." Then I,
"Although the thing that you have hid were evil,
The speaking of it could be no great wrong,
And evil must it be, if done 'twere worse
Than mound and stone that keep all virtue in,
And loosen on us dreams that waste our life,
Shadows and shows that can but turn the brain."
But finding him still silent I stooped down
And whispering that none but he should hear,
Said, "If a woman has put this on you,
My men, whether it please her or displease,
And though they have to cross the Loughlan waters
And take her in the middle of armed men,
Shall make her look upon her handiwork,
That she may quench the rick she has fired; and though
She may have worn silk clothes, or worn a crown,
She'll not be proud, knowing within her heart
That our sufficient portion of the world
Is that we give, although it be brief giving,
Happiness to children and to men."
Then he, driven by his thought beyond his thought,
And speaking what he would not though he would,
Sighed, "You, even you yourself, could work the cure!"
And at those words I rose and I went out
And for nine days he had food from other hands,

And for nine days my mind went whirling round
The one disastrous zodiac, muttering
That the immedicable mound's beyond
Our questioning, beyond our pity even.
But when nine days had gone I stood again
Before his chair and bending down my head
I bade him go when all his household slept
To an old empty woodman's house that's hidden
Westward of Tara, among the hazel-trees –
For hope would give his limbs the power – and await
A friend that could, he had told her, work his cure
And would be no harsh friend.

                 When night had deepened,
I groped my way from beech to hazel wood,
Found that old house, a sputtering torch within,
And stretched out sleeping on a pile of skins
Ardan, and though I called to him and tried
To shake him out of sleep, I could not rouse him.
I waited till the night was on the turn,
Then fearing that some labourer, on his way
To plough or pasture-land, might see me there,
Went out.

           Among the ivy-covered rocks,
As on the blue light of a sword, a man
Who had unnatural majesty, and eyes
Like the eyes of some great kite scouring the woods,
Stood on my path. Trembling from head to foot
I gazed at him like grouse upon a kite;
But with a voice that had unnatural music,
"A weary wooing and a long," he said,
"Speaking of love through other lips and looking
Under the eyelids of another, for it was my craft
That put a passion in the sleeper there,

And when I had got my will and drawn you here,
Where I may speak to you alone, my craft
Sucked up the passion out of him again
And left mere sleep. He'll wake when the sun wakes,
Push out his vigorous limbs and rub his eyes,
And wonder what has ailed him these twelve months."
I cowered back upon the wall in terror,
But that sweet-sounding voice ran on: "Woman,
I was your husband when you rode the air,
Danced in the whirling foam and in the dust,
In days you have not kept in memory,
Being betrayed into a cradle, and I come
That I may claim you as my wife again."
I was no longer terrified – his voice
Had half awakened some old memory –
Yet answered him, "I am King Eochaid's wife
And with him have found every happiness
Women can find." With a most masterful voice,
That made the body seem as it were a string
Under a bow, he cried, "What happiness
Can lovers have that know their happiness
Must end at the dumb stone? But where we build
Our sudden palaces in the still air
Pleasure itself can bring no weariness,
Nor can time waste the cheek, nor is there foot
That has grown weary of the whirling dance,
Nor an unlaughing mouth, but mine that mourns,
Among those mouths that sing their sweethearts' praise,
Your empty bed." "How should I love," I answered,
"Were it not that when the dawn has lit my bed
And shown my husband sleeping there, I have sighed,
'Your strength and nobleness will pass away.'
Or how should love be worth its pains were it not

That when he has fallen asleep within my arms,
Being wearied out, I love in man the child?
What can they know of love that do not know
She builds her nest upon a narrow ledge
Above a windy precipice?" Then he:
"Seeing that when you come to the deathbed
You must return, whether you would or no,
This human life blotted from memory,
Why must I live some thirty, forty years,
Alone with all this useless happiness?"
Thereon he seized me in his arms, but I
Thrust him away with both my hands and cried,
"Never will I believe there is any change
Can blot out of my memory this life
Sweetened by death, but if I could believe,
That were a double hunger in my lips
For what is doubly brief."
                                    And now the shape,
My hands were pressed to, vanished suddenly.
I staggered, but a beech tree stayed my fall,
And clinging to it I could hear the cocks
Crow upon Tara.'
                          King Eochaid bowed his head
And thanked her for her kindness to his brother,
For that she promised, and for that refused.
Thereon the bellowing of the empounded herds
Rose round the walls, and through the bronze-ringed
   door
Jostled and shouted those war-wasted men,
And in the midst King Eochaid's brother stood.
And bade all welcome, being ignorant.

September 1913

What need you, being come to sense,
But fumble in a greasy till
And add the halfpence to the pence
And prayer to shivering prayer, until
You have dried the marrow from the bone?
For men were born to pray and save:
Romantic Ireland's dead and gone,
It's with O'Leary in the grave.

Yet they were of a different kind,
The names that stilled your childish play,
They have gone about the world like wind,
But little time had they to pray
For whom the hangman's rope was spun,
And what, God help us, could they save?
Romantic Ireland's dead and gone,
It's with O'Leary in the grave.

Was it for this the wild geese spread
The grey wing upon every tide;
For this that all that blood was shed,
For this Edward Fitzgerald died,
And Robert Emmet and Wolfe Tone,
All that delirium of the brave?
Romantic Ireland's dead and gone,
It's with O'Leary in the grave.

Yet could we turn the years again,
And call those exiles as they were,
In all their loneliness and pain,
You'd cry, 'Some woman's yellow hair

Has maddened every mother's son':
They weighed so lightly what they gave.
But let them be, they're dead and gone,
They're with O'Leary in the grave.

To a Friend whose work has come to Nothing

Now all the truth is out,
Be secret and take defeat
From any brazen throat,
For how can you compete,
Being honour bred, with one
Who, were it proved he lies,
Were neither shamed in his own
Nor in his neighbours' eyes?
Bred to a harder thing
Than Triumph, turn away
And like a laughing string
Whereon mad fingers play
Amid a place of stone,
Be secret and exult,
Because of all things known
That is most difficult.

Paudeen

Indignant at the fumbling wits, the obscure spite
Of our old Paudeen in his shop, I stumbled blind
Among the stones and thorn-trees, under morning light;
Until a curlew cried and in the luminous wind
A curlew answered; and suddenly thereupon I thought
That on the lonely height where all are in God's eye,
There cannot be, confusion of our sound forgot,
A single soul that lacks a sweet crystaline cry.

To a Shade

If you have revisited the town, thin Shade,
Whether to look upon your monument
(I wonder if the builder has been paid)
Or happier-thoughted when the day is spent
To drink of that salt breath out of the sea
When grey gulls flit about instead of men,
And the gaunt houses put on majesty:
Let these content you and be gone again;
For they are at their old tricks yet.

                      A man
Of your own passionate serving kind who had brought
In his full hands what, had they only known,
Had given their children's children loftier thought,
Sweeter emotion, working in their veins
Like gentle blood, has been driven from the place,
And insult heaped upon him for his pains,
And for his open-handedness, disgrace;
Your enemy, an old foul mouth, had set
The pack upon him.

                 Go, unquiet wanderer,
And gather the Glasnevin coverlet
About your head till the dust stops your ear,
The time for you to taste of that salt breath
And listen at the corners has not come;
You had enough of sorrow before death –
Away, away! You are safer in the tomb.

                      September 29, 1913

When Helen Lived

We have cried in our despair
That men desert,
For some trivial affair
Or noisy, insolent sport,
Beauty that we have won
From bitterest hours;
Yet we, had we walked within
Those topless towers
Where Helen walked with her boy,
Had given but as the rest
Of the men and women of Troy,
A word and a jest.

The Three Beggars

'Though to my feathers in the wet,
I have stood here from break of day,
I have not found a thing to eat
For only rubbish comes my way.
Am I to live on lebeen-lone?'
Muttered the old crane of Gort.
'For all my pains on lebeen-lone.'

King Guare walked amid his court
The palace-yard and river-side
And there to three old beggars said,
'You that have wandered far and wide
Can ravel out what's in my head.
Do men who least desire get most,
Or get the most who most desire? '
A beggar said: 'They get the most
Whom man or devil cannot tire,
And what could make their muscles taut
Unless desire had made them so?'
But Guare laughed with secret thought,
'If that be true as it seems true,
One of you three is a rich man,
For he shall have a thousand pounds
Who is first asleep, if but he can
Sleep before the third noon sounds.'
And thereon merry as a bird,
With his old thoughts King Guare went
From river-side and palace-yard
And left them to their argument.
'And if I win' one beggar said,
'Though I am old I shall persuade

A pretty girl to share my bed';
The second: 'I shall learn a trade';
The third: 'I'll hurry to the course
Among the other gentlemen,
And lay it all upon a horse';
The second: 'I have thought again:
A farmer has more dignity.'
One to another sighed and cried:
The exorbitant dreams of beggary,
That idleness had borne to pride,
Sang through their teeth from noon to noon;
And when the second twilight brought
The frenzy of the beggars' moon
None closed his blood-shot eyes but sought
To keep his fellows from their sleep;
All shouted till their anger grew
Till they were whirling in a heap.

They mauled and bit the whole night through;
They mauled and bit till the day shone;
They mauled and bit through all that day
And till another night had gone,
Or if they made a moment's stay
They sat upon their heels to rail,
And when old Guare came and stood
Before the three to end this tale,
They were commingling lice and blood.
'Time's up,' he cried, and all the three
With blood-shot eyes upon him stared.
'Time's up,' he cried, and all the three
Fell down upon the dust and snored.

'Maybe I shall be lucky yet,
Now they are silent,' said the crane.
'Though to my feathers in the wet
I've stood as I were made of stone
And seen the rubbish run about.
It's certain there are trout somewhere
And maybe I shall take a trout
If but I do not seem to care.'

The Three Hermits

Three old hermits took the air
By a cold and desolate sea,
First was muttering a prayer,
Second rummaged for a flea;
On a windy stone, the third,
Giddy with his hundredth year,
Sang unnoticed like a bird:
'Though the Door of Death is near
And what waits behind the door,
Three times in a single day
I, though upright on the shore,
Fall asleep when I should pray.'
So the first, but now the second:
'We're but given what we have earned
When all thoughts and deeds are reckoned,
So it's plain to be discerned
That the shades of holy men,
Who have failed, being weak of will,
Pass the Door of Birth again,
And are plagued by crowds, until
They've the passion to escape.'
Moaned the other, 'They are thrown
Into some most fearful shape.'
But the second mocked his moan:
'They are not changed to anything,
Having loved God once, but maybe,
To a poet or a king
Or a witty lovely lady.'

While he'd rummaged rags and hair,
Caught and cracked his flea, the third,
Giddy with his hundredth year
Sang unnoticed like a bird.

Beggar to Beggar Cried

'Time to put off the world and go somewhere
And find my health again in the sea air,'
Beggar to beggar cried, being frenzy-struck,
'And make my soul before my pate is bare.'

'And get a comfortable wife and house
To rid me of the devil in my shoes,'
Beggar to beggar cried, being frenzy-struck,
'And the worse devil that is between my thighs.'

'And though I'd marry with a comely lass,
She need not be too comely – let it pass,'
Beggar to beggar cried, being frenzy-struck,
'But there's a devil in a looking-glass.'

'Nor should she be too rich, because the rich
Are driven by wealth as beggars by the itch,'
Beggar to beggar cried, being frenzy-struck,
'And cannot have a humorous happy speech.'

'And there I'll grow respected at my ease,
And hear amid the garden's nightly peace,'
Beggar to beggar cried, being frenzy-struck,
'The wind-blown clamour of the barnacle-geese.'

Running to Paradise

As I came over Windy Gap
They threw a halfpenny into my cap,
For I am running to Paradise;
And all that I need do is to wish
And somebody puts his hand in the dish
To throw me a bit of salted fish:
And there the king is but as the beggar.

My brother Mourteen is worn out
With skelping his big brawling lout,
And I am running to Paradise;
A poor life do what he can,
And though he keep a dog and a gun,
A serving-maid and a serving-man:
And there the king is but as the beggar.

Poor men have grown to be rich men,
And rich men grown to be poor again,
And I am running to Paradise;
And many a darling wit's grown dull
That tossed a bare heel when at school,
Now it has filled an old sock full:
And there the king is but as the beggar.

The wind is old and still at play
While I must hurry upon my way,
For I am running to Paradise;
Yet never have I lit on a friend
To take my fancy like the wind
That nobody can buy or bind:
And there the king is but as the beggar.

The Hour before Dawn

A cursing rogue with a merry face,
A bundle of rags upon a crutch,
Stumbled upon that windy place
Called Cruachan, and it was as much
As the one sturdy leg could do
To keep him upright while he cursed.
He had counted, where long years ago
Queen Maeve's nine Maines had been nursed,
A pair of lapwings, one old sheep,
And not a house to the plain's edge,
When close to his right hand a heap
Of grey stones and a rocky ledge
Reminded him that he could make,
If he but shifted a few stones,
A shelter till the daylight broke.

But while he fumbled with the stones
They toppled over; 'Were it not
I have a lucky wooden shin
I had been hurt'; and toppling brought
Before his eyes, where stones had been,
A dark deep hollow in the rock.
He gave a gasp and thought to have fled,
Being certain it was no right rock
Because an ancient history said
Hell Mouth lay open near that place,
And yet stood still, because inside
A great lad with a beery face
Had tucked himself away beside
A ladle and a tub of beer,
And snored, no phantom by his look.

So with a laugh at his own fear
He crawled into that pleasant nook.

'Night grows uneasy near the dawn
Till even I sleep light; but who
Has tired of his own company?
What one of Maeve's nine brawling sons
Sick of his grave has wakened me?
But let him keep his grave for once
That I may find the sleep I have lost.'

'What care I if you sleep or wake?
But I'll have no man call me ghost.'

'Say what you please, but from daybreak
I'll sleep another century.'

'And I will talk before I sleep
And drink before I talk.'
                                    And he
Had dipped the wooden ladle deep
Into the sleeper's tub of beer
Had not the sleeper started up.

'Before you have dipped it in the beer
I dragged from Goban's mountain-top
I'll have assurance that you are able
To value beer; no half-legged fool
Shall dip his nose into my ladle
Merely for stumbling on this hole
In the bad hour before dawn.'

'Why beer is only beer.'

               'But say
"I'll sleep until the winter's gone,
Or maybe to Midsummer's Day."
And drink, and you will sleep that length.'

'I'd like to sleep till winter's gone,
Or till the sun is in his strength.
This blast has chilled me to the bone.'

'I had no better plan at first.
I thought to wait for that or this.;
Maybe the weather was accursed
Or I had no woman there to kiss;
So slept for half a year or so;
But year by year I found that less
Gave me such pleasure I'd forgo
Even a half-hour's nothingness,
And when at one year's end I found
I had not waked a single minute,
I chose this burrow under ground.
I'll sleep away all time within it:
My sleep were now nine centuries
But for those mornings when I find
The lapwing at their foolish cries
And the sheep bleating at the wind
As when I also played the fool.'

The beggar in a rage began
Upon his hunkers in the hole,
'It's plain that you are no right man
To mock at everything I love
As if it were not worth the doing.
I'd have a merry life enough

If a good Easter wind were blowing
And though the winter wind is bad
I should not be too down in the mouth
For anything you did or said
If but this wind were in the south.'

'You cry aloud, O would 'twere spring
Or that the wind would shift a point,
And do not know that you would bring,
If time were suppler in the joint,
Neither the spring nor the south wind
But the hour when you shall pass away
And leave no smoking wick behind,
For all life longs for the Last Day
And there's no man but cocks his ear
To know when Michael's trumpet cries
That flesh and bone may disappear,
And souls as if they were but sighs,
And there be nothing but God left;
But I alone being blessèd keep
Like some old rabbit to my cleft
And wait Him in a drunken sleep.'
He dipped his ladle in the tub
And drank and yawned and stretched him out.
The other shouted, 'You would rob
My life of every pleasant thought
And every comfortable thing
And so take that and that.' Thereon
He gave him a great pummelling,
But might have pummelled at a stone
For all the sleeper knew or cared;
And after heaped up stone on stone,
And then, grown weary, prayed and cursed

And heaped up stone on stone again,
And prayed and cursed and cursed and fled
From Maeve and all that juggling plain,
Nor gave God thanks till overhead
The clouds were brightening with the dawn.

A Song from 'The Player Queen'

My mother dandled me and sang,
'How young it is, how young!'
And made a golden cradle
That on a willow swung.

'He went away,' my mother sang,
'When I was brought to bed,'
And all the while her needle pulled
The gold and silver thread.

She pulled the thread and bit the thread
And made a golden gown,
And wept because she had dreamt that I
Was born to wear a crown.

'When she was got,' my mother sang,
'I heard a sea-mew cry,
And saw a flake of the yellow foam
That dropped upon my thigh.'

How therefore could she help but braid
The gold into my hair,
And dream that I should carry
The golden top of care?

The Mountain Tomb

Pour wine and dance if manhood still have pride,
Bring roses if the rose be yet in bloom;
The cataract smokes upon the mountain side,
Our Father Rosicross is in his tomb.

Pull down the blinds, bring fiddle and clarionet
That there be no foot silent in the room
Nor mouth from kissing, nor from wine unwet;
Our Father Rosicross is in his tomb.

In vain, in vain; the cataract still cries
The everlasting taper lights the gloom;
All wisdom shut into his onyx eyes,
Our Father Rosicross sleeps in his tomb.

To a Child Dancing in the Wind

I

Dance there upon the shore;
What need have you to care
For wind or water's roar?
And tumble out your hair
That the salt drops have wet;
Being young you have not known
The fool's triumph, nor yet
Love lost as soon as won,
Nor the best labourer dead
And all the sheaves to bind.
What need have you to dread
The monstrous crying of wind?

II

Has no one said those daring
Kind eyes should be more learn'd?
Or warned you how despairing
The moths are when they are burned?
I could have warned you, but you are young,
So we speak a different tongue.

O you will take whatever's offered
And dream that all the world's a friend,
Suffer as your mother suffered,
Be as broken in the end.
But I am old and you are young,
And I speak a barbarous tongue.

A Memory of Youth

The moments passed as at a play;
I had the wisdom love brings forth;
I had my share of mother-wit,
And yet for all that I could say,
And though I had her praise for it,
A cloud blown from the cut-throat north
Suddenly hid Love's moon away.

Believing every word I said,
I praised her body and her mind
Till pride had made her eyes grow bright,
And pleasure made her cheeks grow red,
And vanity her footfall light,
Yet we, for all that praise, could find
Nothing but darkness overhead.

We sat as silent as a stone,
We knew, though she'd not said a word,
That even the best of love must die,
And had been savagely undone
Were it not that Love upon the cry
Of a most ridiculous little bird
Tore from the clouds his marvellous moon.

Fallen Majesty

Although crowds gathered once if she but showed her
    face,
And even old men's eyes grew dim, this hand alone,
Like some last courtier at a gypsy camping place,
Babbling of fallen majesty, records what's gone.

The lineaments, a heart that laughter has made sweet,
These, these remain, but I record what's gone. A crowd
Will gather, and not know it walks the very street
Whereon a thing once walked that seemed a burning
    cloud.

His Dream

I swayed upon the gaudy stern
The butt-end of a steering-oar,
And saw wherever I could turn
A crowd upon a shore.

And though I would have hushed the crowd,
There was no mother's son but said,
'What is the figure in a shroud
Upon a gaudy bed?'

And after running at the brim
Cried out upon that thing beneath,
– It had such dignity of limb, –
By the sweet name of Death.

Though I'd my finger on my lip,
What could I but take up the song?
And runnung crowd and gaudy ship
Cried out the whole night long,

Crying amid the glittering sea,
Naming it with ecstatic breath,
Because it had such dignity,
By the sweet name of Death.

Friends

Now must I these three praise –
Three women that have wrought
What joy is in my days;
One because no thought,
Nor those unpassing cares,
No, not in these fifteen
Many-times-troubled years,
Could ever come between
Mind and delighted mind;
And one because her hand
Had strength that could unbind
What none can understand,
What none can have and thrive,
Youth's dreamy load, till she
So changed me that I live
Labouring in ecstasy.
And what of her that took
All till my youth was gone
With scarce a pitying look?
How should I praise that one?
When day begins to break
I count my good and bad,
Being wakeful for her sake,
Remembering what she had,
What eagle look still shows,
While up from my heart's root
So great a sweetness flows
I shake from head to foots.

The Cold Heaven

Suddenly I saw the cold and rook-delighting heaven
That seemed as though ice burned and was but the more
   ice,
And thereupon imagination and heart were driven
So wild that every casual thought of that and this
Vanished, and left but memories, that should be out of
   season
With the hot blood of youth, of love crossed long ago;
And I took all the blame out of all sense and reason,
Until I cried and trembled and rocked to and fro,
Riddled with light. Ah! when the ghost begins to quicken,
Confusion of the death-bed over, is it sent
Out naked on the roads, as the books say, and stricken
By the injustice of the skies for punishment?

That the Night Come

She lived in storm and strife,
Her soul had such desire
For what proud death may bring
That it could not endure
The common good of life,
But lived as 'twere a king
That packed his marriage day
With banneret and pennon,
Trumpet and kettledrum,
And the outrageous cannon,
To bundle time away
That the night come.

The Magi

Now as at all times I can see in the mind's eye,
In their stiff, painted clothes, the pale unsatisfied ones
Appear and disappear in the blue depth of the sky
With all their ancient faces like rain-beaten stones,
And all their helms of silver hovering side by side,
And all their eyes still fixed, hoping to find once more,
Being by Calvary's turbulence unsatisfied,
The uncontrollable mystery on the bestial floor.

A Coat

I made my song a coat
Covered with embroideries
Out of old mythologies
From heel to throat;
But the fools caught it,
Wore it in the world's eyes
As though they'd wrought it.
Song, let them take it
For there's more enterprise
In walking naked.

The Wild Swans at Coole

The trees are in their autumn beauty,
The woodland paths are dry,
Under the October twilight the water
Mirrors a still sky;
Upon the brimming water among the stones
Are nine and fifty swans.

The nineteenth autumn has come upon me
Since I first made my count;
I saw, before I had well finished,
All suddenly mount
And scatter wheeling in great broken rings
Upon their clamorous wings.

I have looked upon those brilliant creatures,
And now my heart is sore.
All's changed since I, hearing at twilight,
The first time on this shore,
The bell-beat of their wings above my head,
Trod with a lighter tread.

Unwearied still, lover by lover,
They paddle in the cold,
Companionable streams or climb the air;
Their hearts have not grown old;
Passion or conquest, wander where they will,
Attend upon them still.

But now they drift on the still water
Mysterious, beautiful;

Among what rushes will they build,
By what lake's edge or pool
Delight men's eyes, when I awake some day
To find they have flown away?

An Irish Airman Foresees his Death

I know that I shall meet my fate
Somewhere among the clouds above;
Those that I fight I do not hate
Those that I guard I do not love;
My country is Kiltartan Cross,
My countrymen Kiltartan's poor,
No likely end could bring them loss
Or leave them happier than before.
Nor law, nor duty bade me fight,
Nor public man, nor cheering crowds,
A lonely impulse of delight
Drove to this tumult in the clouds;
I balanced all, brought all to mind,
The years to come seemed waste of breath,
A waste of breath the years behind
In balance with this life, this death.

Men Improve with the Years

I am worn out with dreams;
A weather-worn, marble triton
Among the streams;
And all day long I look
Upon this lady's beauty
As though I had found in book
A pictured beauty,
Pleased to have filled the eyes
Or the discerning ears,
Delighted to be but wise,
For men improve with the years;
And yet and yet
Is this my dream, or the truth?
O would that we had met
When I had my burning youth;
But I grow old among dreams,
A weather-worn, marble triton
Among the streams.

Under the Round Tower

'Although I'd lie lapped up in linen
A deal I'd sweat and little earn
If I should live as live the neighbours,'
Cried the beggar, Billy Byrne;
'Stretch bones till the daylight come
On great-grandfather's battered tomb.'

Upon a grey old battered tombstone
In Glendalough beside the stream,
Where the O'Byrnes and Byrnes are buried,
He stretched his bones and fell in a dream
Of sun and moon that a good hour
Bellowed and pranced in the round tower;

Of golden king and silver lady,
Bellowing up and bellowing round,
Till toes mastered a sweet measure,
Mouth mastered a sweet sound,
Prancing round and prancing up
Until they pranced upon the top.

That golden king and that wild lady
Sang till stars began to fade,
Hands gripped in hands, toes close together,
Hair spread on the wind they made;
That lady and that golden king
Could like a brace of blackbirds sing.

'It's certain that my luck is broken,'
That rambling jailbird Billy said;

'Before nightfall I'll pick a pocket
And snug it in a feather-bed,
I cannot find the peace of home
On great-grandfather's battered tomb.'

Solomon to Sheba

Sang Solomon to Sheba,
And kissed her dusky face,
'All day long from mid-day
We have talked in the one place,
All day long from shadowless noon
We have gone round and round
In the narrow theme of love
Like an old horse in a pound.'

To Solomon sang Sheba,
Planted on his knees,
'If you had broached a matter
That might the learned please,
You had before the sun had thrown
Our shadows on the ground
Discovered that my thoughts, not it,
Are but a narrow pound.'

Sang Solomon to Sheba,
And kissed her Arab eyes,
'There's not a man or woman
Born under the skies
Dare match in learning with us two,
And all day long we have found
There's not a thing but love can make
The world a narrow pound.'

The Living Beauty

I bade, because the wick and oil are spent
And frozen are the channels of the blood,
My discontented heart to draw content
From beauty that is cast out of a mould
In bronze, or that in dazzling marble appears,
Appears, but when we have gone is gone again,
Being more indifferent to our solitude
Than 'twere an apparition. O heart, we are old,
The living beauty is for younger men,
We cannot pay its tribute of wild tears.

The Scholars

Bald heads forgetful of their sins,
Old, learned, respectable bald heads
Edit and annotate the lines
That young men, tossing on their beds,
Rhymed out in love's despair
To flatter beauty's ignorant ear.

All shuffle there; all cough in the ink;
All wear the carpet with their shoes;
All think what other people think;
All know the man their neighbour knows.
Lord, what would they say
Did their Catullus walk that way?

The Fisherman

Although I can see him still,
The freckled man who goes
To a grey place on a hill
In grey Connemara clothes
At dawn to cast his flies,
It's long since I began
To call up to the eyes
This wise and simple man.
All day I'd looked in the face
What I had hoped 'twould be
To write for my own race
And the reality;
The living men that I hate,
The dead man that I loved,
The craven man in his seat,
The insolent unreproved,
And no knave brought to book
Who has won a drunken cheer,
The witty man and his joke
Aimed at the commonest ear,
The clever man who cries
The catch-cries of the clown,
The beating down of the wise
And great Art beaten down.

Maybe a twelvemonth since
Suddenly I began,
In scorn of this audience,
Imagining a man,
And his sun-freckled face,
And grey Connemara cloth,

Climbing up to a place
Where stone is dark under froth,
And the down-turn of his wrist
When the flies drop in the stream:
A man who does not exist,
A man who is but a dream;
And cried, 'Before I am old
I shall have written him one
Poem maybe as cold
And passionate as the dawn.'

The Hawk

'Call down the hawk from the air;
Let him be hooded or caged
Till the yellow eye has grown mild,
For larder and spit are bare,
The old cook enraged,
The scullion gone wild.'

'I will not be clapped in a hood,
Nor a cage, nor alight upon wrist,
Now I have learnt to be proud
Hovering over the wood
In the broken mist
Or tumbling cloud.'

'What tumbling cloud did you cleave,
Yellow-eyed hawk of the mind,
Last evening? that I, who had sat
Dumbfounded before a knave,
Should give to my friend
A pretence of wit.'

Her Praise

She is foremost of those that I would hear praised.
I have gone about the house, gone up and down
As a man does who has published a new book,
Or a young girl dressed out in her new gown,
And though I have turned the talk by hook or crook
Until her praise should be the uppermost theme,
A woman spoke of some new tale she had read,
A man confusedly in a half dream
As though some other name ran in his head.
She is foremost of those that I would hear praised.
I will talk no more of books or the long war
But walk by the dry thorn until I have found
Some beggar sheltering from the wind, and there
Manage the talk until her name come round.
If there be rags enough he will know her name
And be well pleased remembering it, for in the old days,
Though she had young men's praise and old men's blame,
Among the poor both old and young gave her praise.

The People

'What have I earned for all that work,' I said,
'For all that I have done at my own charge?
The daily spite of this unmannerly town,
Where who has served the most is most defamed,
The reputation of his lifetime lost
Between the night and morning. I might have lived,
And you know well how great the longing has been,
Where every day my footfall should have lit
In the green shadow of Ferrara wall;
Or climbed among the images of the past –
The unperturbed and courtly images –
Evening and morning, the steep street of Urbino
To where the Duchess and her people talked
The stately midnight through until they stood
In their great window looking at the dawn;
I might have had no friend that could not mix
Courtesy and passion into one like those
That saw the wicks grow yellow in the dawn;
I might have used the one substantial right
My trade allows: chosen my company,
And chosen what scenery had pleased me best.'
Thereon my phoenix answered in reproof,
'The drunkards, pilferers of public funds,
All the dishonest crowd I had driven away,
When my luck changed and they dared meet my face,
Crawled from obscurity, and set upon me
Those I had served and some that I had fed;
Yet never have I, now nor any time,
Complained of the people.'

                    All I could reply
Was: 'You, that have not lived in thought but deed,
Can have the purity of a natural force,
But I, whose virtues are the definitions
Of the analytic mind, can neither close
The eye of the mind nor keep my tongue from speech.'
And yet, because my heart leaped at her words,
I was abashed, and now they come to mind
After nine years, I sink my head abashed.

His Phoenix

There is a queen in China, or maybe it's in Spain,
And birthdays and holidays such praises can be heard
Of her unblemished lineaments, a whiteness with no
  stain,
That she might be that sprightly girl who was trodden by
  a bird;
And there's a score of duchesses, surpassing womankind,
Or who have found a painter to make them so for pay
And smooth out stain and blemish with the elegance of
  his mind:
I knew a phoenix in my youth, so let them have their day.

The young men every night applaud their Gaby's laughing
  eye,
And Ruth St Denis had more charm although she had
  poor luck;
From nineteen hundred nine or ten, Pavlova's had the cry
And there's a player in the States who gathers up her cloak
And flings herself out of the room when Juliet would be
  bride
With all a woman's passion, a child's imperious way,
And there are — but no matter if there are scores beside:
I knew a phoenix in my youth, so let them have their day.

There's Margaret and Marjorie and Dorothy and Nan,
A Daphne and a Mary who live in privacy;
One's had her fill of lovers, another's had but one,
Another boasts, 'I pick and choose and have but two or
  three.'
If head and limb have beauty and the instep's high and
  light,

They can spread out what sail they please for all I have to
say,
Be but the breakers of men's hearts or engines of delight:
I knew a phoenix in my youth, so let them have their day.

There'll be that crowd to make men wild through all the
centuries,
And maybe there'll be some young belle walk out to
make men wild
Who is my beauty's equal, though that my heart denies,
But not the exact likeness, the simplicity of a child,
And that proud look as though she had gazed into the
burning sun,
And all the shapely body no tittle gone astray,
I mourn for that most lonely thing; and yet God's will be
done,
I knew a phoenix in my youth so let them have their day.

Broken Dreams

There is grey in your hair.
Young men no longer suddenly catch their breath
When you are passing;
But maybe some old gaffer mutters a blessing
Because it was your prayer
Recovered him upon the bed of death.
For your sole sake – that all heart's ache have known,
And given to others all heart's ache,
From meagre girlhood's putting on
Burdensome beauty – for your sole sake
Heaven has put away the stroke of her doom,
So great her portion in that peace you make
By merely walking in a room.

Your beauty can but leave among us
Vague memories, nothing but memories.
A young man when the old men are done talking
Will say to an old man, 'Tell me of that lady
The poet stubborn with his passion sang us
When age might well have chilled his blood.'

Vague memories, nothing but memories,
But in the grave all, all, shall be renewed.
The certainty that I shall see that lady
Leaning or standing or walking
In the first loveliness of womanhood,
And with the fervour of my youthful eyes,
Has set me muttering like a fool.

You are more beautiful than any one,
And yet your body had a flaw:

Your small hands were not beautiful,
And I am afraid that you will run
And paddle to the wrist
In that mysterious, always brimming lake
Where those that have obeyed the holy law
Paddle and are perfect; leave unchanged
The hands that I have kissed,
For old sakes' sake.

The last stroke of midnight dies.
All day in the one chair
From dream to dream and rhyme to rhyme I have ranged
In rambling talk with an image of air:
Vague memories, nothing but memories.

On being asked for a War Poem

I think it better that in times like these
A poet's mouth be silent, for in truth
We have no gift to set a statesman right;
He has had enough of meddling who can please
A young girl in the indolence of her youth,
Or an old man upon a winter's night.

Ego Dominus Tuus

Hic. On the grey sand beside the shallow stream
   Under your old wind-beaten tower, where still
   A lamp burns on beside the open book
   That Michael Robartes left, you walk in the moon,
   And, though you have passed the best of life, still trace
   Enthralled by the unconquerable delusion,
   Magical shapes.

Ille.   By the help of an image
   I call to my own opposite, summon all
   That I have handled least, least looked upon.

Hic. And I would find myself and not an image.

Ille. That is our modern hope, and by its light
   We have lit upon the gentle, sensitive mind
   And lost the old nonchalance of the hand;
   Whether we have chosen chisel, pen or brush
   We are but critics, or but half create,
   Timid, entangled, empty and abashed
   Lacking the countenance of our friends.

Hic.   And yet
   The chief imagination of Christendom
   Dante Alighieri, so utterly found himself
   That he has made that hollow face of his
   More plain to the mind's eye than any face
   But that of Christ.

Ille.   And did he find himself
   Or was the hunger that had made it hollow

A hunger for the apple on the bough
Most out of reach? and is that spectral image
The man that Lapo and that Guido knew?
I think he fashioned from his opposite
An image that might have been a stony face,
Staring upon a Bedouin's horse-hair roof
From doored and windowed cliff, or half upturned
Among the coarse grass and the camel dung.
He set his chisel to the hardest stone.
Being mocked by Guido for his lecherous life,
Derided and deriding, driven out
To climb that stair and eat that bitter bread,
He found the unpersuadable justice, he found
The most exalted lady loved by a man.

Hic. Yet surely there are men who have made their art
    Out of no tragic war, lovers of life,
    Impulsive men that look for happiness
    And sing when they have found it.

Ille.   No, not sing,
    For those that love the world serve it in action,
    Grow rich, popular and full of influence,
    And should they paint or write still it is action:
    The struggle of the fly in marmalade.
    The rhetorician would deceive his neighbours,
    The sentimentalist himself; while art
    Is but a vision of reality.
    What portion in the world can the artist have
    Who has awakened from the common dream
    But dissipation and despair?

Hic.   And yet
  No one denies to Keats love of the world;
  Remember his deliberate happiness.

Ille. His art is happy, but who knows his mind?
  I see a schoolboy when I think of him,
  With face and nose pressed to a sweet-shop window,
  For certainly he sank into his grave
  His senses and his heart unsatisfied,
  And made – being poor, ailing and ignorant,
  Shut out from all the luxury of the world,
  The coarse-bred son of a livery stablekeeper –
  Luxuriant song.

Hic.   Why should you leave the lamp
  Burning alone beside an open book.
  And trace these characters upon the sands?
  A style is found by sedentary toil
  And by the imitation of great masters.

Ille. Because I seek an image, not a book.
  Those men that in their writings are most wise
  Own nothing but their blind, stupefied hearts.
  I call to the mysterious one who yet
  Shall walk the wet sands by the edge of the stream
  And look most like me, being indeed my double,
  And prove of all imaginable things
  The most unlike, being my anti-self,
  And standing by these characters disclose
  All that I seek; and whisper it as though
  He were afraid the birds, who cry aloud
  Their momentary cries before it is dawn,
  Would carry it away to blasphemous men.

The Cat and the Moon

The cat went here and there
And the moon spun round like a top,
And the nearest kin of the moon,
The creeping cat, looked up.
Black Minnaloushe stared at the moon,
For, wander and wail as he would,
The pure cold light in the sky
Troubled his animal blood.
Minnaloushe runs in the grass,
Lifting his delicate feet.
Do you dance, Minnaloushe, do you dance?
When two close kindred meet,
What better than call a dance?
Maybe the moon may learn,
Tired of that courtly fashion,
A new dance turn.
Minnaloushe creeps through the grass
From moonlit place to place,
The sacred moon overhead
Has taken a new phase.
Does Minnaloushe know that his pupils
Will pass from change to change,
And that from round to crescent,
From crescent to round they range?
Minnaloushe creeps through the grass
Alone, important and wise,
And lifts to the changing moon
His changing eyes.

Two Songs of a Fool

I

A speckled cat and a tame hare
Eat at my hearthstone
And sleep there;
And both look up to me alone
For learning and defence
As I look up to Providence.

I start out of my sleep to think
Some day I may forget
Their food and drink;
Or, the house door left unshut,
The hare may run till it's found
The horn's sweet note and the tooth of the hound.

I bear a burden that might well try
Men that do all by rule,
And what can I
That am a wandering witted fool
But pray to God that He ease
My great responsibilities.

II

I slept on my three-legged stool by the fire.
The speckled cat slept on my knee;
We never thought to enquire
Where the brown hare might be,
And whether the door were shut.
Who knows how she drank the wind
Stretched up on two legs from the mat,
Before she had settled her mind

To drum with her heel and to leap?
Had I but awakened from sleep
And called her name, she had heard,
It may be, and had not stirred,
That now, it may be, has found
The horn's sweet note and the tooth of the hound.

A Prayer on going into my House

God grant a blessing on this tower and cottage
And on my heirs, if all remain unspoiled,
No table or chair or stool not simple enough
For shepherd lads in Galilee; and grant
That I myself for portions of the year
May handle nothing and set eyes on nothing
But what the great and passionate have used
Throughout so many varying centuries.
We take it for the norm; yet should I dream
Sinbad the sailor's brought a painted chest,
Or image, from beyond the Loadstone Mountain,
That dream is a norm; and should some limb of the
    Devil
Destroy the view by cutting down an ash
That shades the road, or setting up a cottage
Planned in a government office, shorten his life,
Manacle his soul upon the Red Sea bottom.

The Saint and the Hunchback

Hunchback. Stand up and lift your hand and bless
A man that finds great bitterness
In thinking of his lost renown.
A Roman Caesar is held down
Under this hump.

Saint.   God tries each man
According to a different plan.
I shall not cease to bless because
I lay about me with the taws
That night and morning I may thrash
Greek Alexander from my flesh,
Augustus Caesar, and after these
That great rogue Alcibiades.

Hunchback. To all that in your flesh have stood
And blessed, I give my gratitude,
Honoured by all in their degrees,
But most to Alcibiades.

The Double Vision of Michael Robartes

I

On the grey rock of Cashel the mind's eye
Has called up the cold spirits that are born
When the old moon is vanished from the sky
And the new still hides her horn.

Under blank eyes and fingers never still
The particular is pounded till it is man.
When had I my own will?
O, not since life began.

Constrained, arraigned, baffled, bent and unbent
By these wire-jointed jaws and limbs of wood,
Themselves obedient,
Knowing not evil and good;

Obedient to some hidden magical breath.
They do not even feel, so abstract are they,
So dead beyond our death,
Triumph that we obey.

II

On the grey rock of Cashel I suddenly saw
A Sphinx with woman breast and lion paw,
A Buddha, hand at rest,
Hand lifted up that blest;

And right between these two a girl at play
That, it may be, had danced her life away,
For now being dead it seemed
That she of dancing dreamed.

Although I saw it all in the mind's eye
There can be nothing solider till I die;
I saw by the moon's light
Now at its fifteenth night.

One lashed her tail; her eyes lit by the moon
Gazed upon all things known, all things unknown,
In triumph of intellect
With motionless head erect.

That other's moonlit eyeballs never moved,
Being fixed on all things loved, all things unloved.
Yet little peace he had,
For those that love are sad.

O little did they care who danced between,
And little she by whom her dance was seen
So she danced. No thought,
Body perfection brought,

For what but eye and ear silence the mind
With the minute particulars of mankind?
Mind moved yet seemed to stop
As 'twere a spinning-top.

In contemplation had those three so wrought
Upon a moment, and so stretched it out
That they, time overthrown,
Were dead yet flesh and bone.

III

I knew that I had seen, had seen at last
That girl my unremembering nights hold fast
Or else my dreams that fly
If I should rub an eye,

And yet in flying fling into my meat
A crazy juice that makes the pulses beat
As though I had been undone
By Homer's Paragon

Who never gave the burning town a thought;
To such a pitch of folly I am brought,
Being caught between the pull
Of the dark moon and the full,

The commonness of thought and images
That have the frenzy of our western seas.
Thereon I made my moan,
And after kissed a stone,

And after that arranged it in a song
Seeing that I, ignorant for so long,
Had been rewarded thus
In Cormac's ruined house.

Michael Robartes and the Dancer

He. Opinion is not worth a rush;
  In this altar-piece the knight,
  Who grips his long spear so to push
  That dragon through the fading light,
  Loved the lady; and it's plain
  The half-dead dragon was her thought,
  That every morning rose again
  And dug its claws and shrieked and fought.
  Could the impossible come to pass
  She would have time to turn her eyes,
  Her lover thought, upon the glass
  And on the instant would grow wise.

She. You mean they argued.

He.   Put it so;
  But bear in mind your lover's wage
  Is what your looking-glass can show,
  And that he will turn green with rage
  At all that is not pictured there.

She. May I not put myself to college?

He. Go pluck Athene by the hair;
  For what mere book can grant a knowledge
  With an impassioned gravity
  Appropriate to that beating breast,
  That vigorous thigh, that dreaming eye?
  And may the Devil take the rest.

She. And must no beautiful woman be
    Learned like a man?

He.   Paul Veronese
    And all his sacred company
    Imagined bodies all their days
    By the lagoon you love so much,
    For proud, soft, ceremonious proof
    That all must come to sight and touch;
    While Michael Angelo's Sistine roof,
    His "Morning' and his "Night' disclose
    How sinew that has been pulled tight,
    Or it may be loosened in repose,
    Can rule by supernatural right
    Yet be but sinew.

She.   I have heard said
    There is great danger in the body.

He. Did God in portioning wine and bread
    Give man His thought or His mere body?

She. My wretched dragon is perplexed.

He. I have principles to prove me right.
    It follows from this Latin text
    That blest souls are not composite,
    And that all beautiful women may
    Live in uncomposite blessedness,
    And lead us to the like – if they
    Will banish every thought, unless
    The lineaments that please their view

When the long looking-glass is full,
Even from the foot-sole think it too.

She. They say such different things at school.

Solomon and the Witch

And thus declared that Arab lady:
'Last night, where under the wild moon
On grassy mattress I had laid me,
Within my arms great Solomon,
I suddenly cried out in a strange tongue
Not his, not mine.'
                   Who understood
Whatever has been said, sighed, sung,
Howled, miau-d, barked, brayed, belled, yelled, cried,
   crowed,
Thereon replied: 'A cockerel
Crew from a blossoming apple bough
Three hundred years before the Fall,
And never crew again till now,
And would not now but that he thought,
Chance being at one with Choice at last,
All that the brigand apple brought
And this foul world were dead at last.
He that crowed out eternity
Thought to have crowed it in again.
For though love has a spider's eye
To find out some appropriate pain —
Aye, though all passion's in the glance —
For every nerve, and tests a lover
With cruelties of Choice and Chance;
And when at last that murder's over
Maybe the bride-bed brings despair,
For each an imagined image brings
And finds a real image there;
Yet the world ends when these two things,
Though several, are a single light,

When oil and wick are burned in one;
Therefore a blessed moon last night
Gave Sheba to her Solomon.'

'Yet the world stays.'
                              'If that be so,
Your cockerel found us in the wrong
Although he thought it worth a crow.
Maybe an image is too strong
Or maybe is not strong enough.'

'The night has fallen; not a sound
In the forbidden sacred grove
Unless a petal hit the ground,
Nor any human sight within it
But the crushed grass where we have lain!
And the moon is wilder every minute.
O! Solomon! let us try again.'

An Image from a Past Life

He. Never until this night have I been stirred.
   The elaborate starlight throws a reflection
   On the dark stream,
   Till all the eddies gleam;
   And thereupon there comes that scream
   From terrified, invisible beast or bird:
   Image of poignant recollection.

She. An image of my heart that is smitten through
   Out of all likelihood, or reason,
   And when at last,
   Youth's bitterness being past,
   I had thought that all my days were cast
   Amid most lovely places; smitten as though
   It had not learned its lesson.

He. Why have you laid your hands upon my eyes?
   What can have suddenly alarmed you
   Whereon 'twere best
   My eyes should never rest?
   What is there but the slowly fading west,
   The river imaging the flashing skies,
   All that to this moment charmed you?

She. A sweetheart from another life floats there
   As though she had been forced to linger
   From vague distress
   Or arrogant loveliness,
   Merely to loosen out a tress
   Among the starry eddies of her hair
   Upon the paleness of a finger.

He. But why should you grow suddenly afraid
   And start — I at your shoulder —
   Imagining
   That any night could bring
   An image up, or anything
   Even to eyes that beauty had driven mad,
   But images to make me fonder?

She. Now she has thrown her arms above her head;
   Whether she threw them up to flout me,
   Or but to find,
   Now that no fingers bind,
   That her hair streams upon the wind,
   I do not know, that know I am afraid
   Of the hovering thing night brought me.

Under Saturn

Do not because this day I have grown saturnine
Imagine that lost love, inseparable from my thought
Because I have no other youth, can make me pine;
For how should I forget the wisdom that you brought,
The comfort that you made? Although my wits have gone
On a fantastic ride, my horse's flanks are spurred
By childish memories of an old cross Pollexfen,
And of a Middleton, whose name you never heard,
And of a red-haired Yeats whose looks, although he died
Before my time, seem like a vivid memory.
You heard that labouring man who had served my people.
  He said
Upon the open road, near to the Sligo quay –
No, no, not said, but cried it out – 'You have come again
And surely after twenty years it was time to come.'
I am thinking of a child's vow sworn in vain
Never to leave that valley his fathers called their home.

Easter, 1916

I have met them at close of day
Coming with vivid faces
From counter or desk among grey
Eighteenth-century houses.
I have passed with a nod of the head
Or polite meaningless words,
Or have lingered awhile and said
Polite meaningless words,
And thought before I had done
Of a mocking tale or a gibe
To please a companion
Around the fire at the club,
Being certain that they and I
But lived where motley is worn:
All changed, changed utterly:
A terrible beauty is born.

That woman's days were spent
In ignorant good will,
Her nights in argument
Until her voice grew shrill.
What voice more sweet than hers
When, young and beautiful,
She rode to harriers?
This man had kept a school
And rode our wingèd horse;
This other his helper and friend
Was coming into his force;
He might have won fame in the end,
So sensitive his nature seemed,
So daring and sweet his thought.

This other man I had dreamed
A drunken, vainglorious lout.
He had done most bitter wrong
To some who are near my heart,
Yet I number him in the song;
He, too, has resigned his part
In the casual comedy;
He, too, has been changed in his turn,
Transformed utterly:
A terrible beauty is born.

Hearts with one purpose alone
Through summer and winter seem
Enchanted to a stone
To trouble the living stream.
The horse that comes from the road,
The rider, the birds that range
From cloud to tumbling cloud,
Minute by minute they change;
A shadow of cloud on the stream
Changes minute by minute;
A horse-hoof slides on the brim,
And a horse plashes within it;
Where long-legged moor-hens dive,
And hens to moor-cocks call.
Minute by minute they live:
The stone's in the midst of all.

Too long a sacrifice
Can make a stone of the heart.
O when may it suffice?
That is heaven's part, our part
To murmur name upon name,

As a mother names her child
When sleep at last has come
On limbs that had run wild.
What is it but nightfall?
No, no, not night but death;
Was it needless death after all?
For England may keep faith
For all that is done and said.
We know their dream; enough
To know they dreamed and are dead;
And what if excess of love
Bewildered them till they died?
I write it out in a verse —
MacDonagh and MacBride
And Connolly and Pearse
Now and in time to be,
Wherever green is worn,
Are changed, changed utterly:
A terrible beauty is born.

Sixteen Dead Men

O but we talked at large before
The sixteen men were shot,
But who can talk of give and take,
What should be and what not
While those dead men are loitering there
To stir the boiling pot?

You say that we should still the land
Till Germany's overcome;
But who is there to argue that
Now Pearse is deaf and dumb?
And is their logic to outweigh
MacDonagh's bony thumb?

How could you dream they'd listen
That have an ear alone
For those new comrades they have found,
Lord Edward and Wolfe Tone,
Or meddle with our give and take
That converse bone to bone?

The Leaders of the Crowd

They must to keep their certainty accuse
All that are different of a base intent;
Pull down established honour; hawk for news
Whatever their loose fantasy invent
And murmur it with bated breath, as though
The abounding gutter had been Helicon
Or calumny a song. How can they know
Truth flourishes where the student's lamp has shone,
And there alone, that have no solitude?
So the crowd come they care not what may come.
They have loud music, hope every day renewed
And heartier loves; that lamp is from the tomb.

Demon and Beast

For certain minutes at the least
That crafty demon and that loud beast
That plague me day and night
Ran out of my sight;
Though I had long perned in the gyre,
Between my hatred and desire,
I saw my freedom won
And all laugh in the sun.

The glittering eyes in a death's head
Of old Luke Wadding's portrait said
Welcome, and the Ormondes all
Nodded upon the wall,
And even Strafford smiled as though
It made him happier to know
I understood his plan.
Now that the loud beast ran
There was no portrait in the Gallery
But beckoned to sweet company,
For all men's thoughts grew clear
Being dear as mine are dear.

But soon a tear-drop started up,
For aimless joy had made me stop
Beside the little lake
To watch a white gull take
A bit of bread thrown up into the air;
Now gyring down and perning there
He splashed where an absurd
Portly green-pated bird
Shook off the water from his back;

Being no more demoniac
A stupid happy creature
Could rouse my whole nature.

Yet I am certain as can be
That every natural victory
Belongs to beast or demon,
That never yet had freeman
Right mastery of natural things,
And that mere growing old, that brings
Chilled blood, this sweetness brought;
Yet have no dearer thought
Than that I may find out a way
To make it linger half a day.

O what a sweetness strayed
Through barren Thebaid,
Or by the Mareotic sea
When that exultant Anthony
And twice a thousand more
Starved upon the shore
And withered to a bag of bones!
What had the Caesars but their thrones?

The Second Coming

Turning and turning in the widening gyre
The falcon cannot hear the falconer;
Things fall apart; the centre cannot hold;
Mere anarchy is loosed upon the world,
The blood-dimmed tide is loosed, and everywhere
The ceremony of innocence is drowned;
The best lack all conviction, while the worst
Are full of passionate intensity.

Surely some revelation is at hand;
Surely the Second Coming is at hand.
The Second Coming! Hardly are those words out
When a vast image out of *Spiritus Mundi*
Troubles my sight: somewhere in sands of the desert
A shape with lion body and the head of a man,
A gaze blank and pitiless as the sun,
Is moving its slow thighs, while all about it
Reel shadows of the indignant desert birds.
The darkness drops again; but now I know
That twenty centuries of stony sleep
Were vexed to nightmare by a rocking cradle,
And what rough beast, its hour come round at last,
Slouches towards Bethlehem to be born?

A Prayer for my Daughter

Once more the storm is howling, and half hid
Under this cradle-hood and coverlid
My child sleeps on. There is no obstacle
But Gregory's wood and one bare hill
Whereby the haystack – and roof-levelling wind,
Bred on the Atlantic, can be stayed;
And for an hour I have walked and prayed
Because of the great gloom that is in my mind.

I have walked and prayed for this young child an hour
And heard the sea-wind scream upon the tower,
And under the arches of the bridge, and scream
In the elms above the flooded stream;
Imagining in excited reverie
That the future years had come,
Dancing to a frenzied drum,
Out of the murderous innocence of the sea.

May she be granted beauty and yet not
Beauty to make a stranger's eye distraught,
Or hers before a looking-glass, for such,
Being made beautiful overmuch,
Consider beauty a sufficient end,
Lose natural kindness and maybe
The heart-revealing intimacy
That chooses right, and never find a friend.

Helen being chosen found life flat and dull
And later had much trouble from a fool,
While that great Queen, that rose out of the spray,
Being fatherless could have her way

Yet chose a bandy-legged smith for man.
It's certain that fine women eat
A crazy salad with their meat
Whereby the Horn of plenty is undone.

In courtesy I'd have her chiefly learned;
Hearts are not had as a gift but hearts are earned
By those that are not entirely beautiful;
Yet many, that have played the fool
For beauty's very self, has charm made wise.
And many a poor man that has roved,
Loved and thought himself beloved,
From a glad kindness cannot take his eyes.

May she become a flourishing hidden tree
That all her thoughts may like the linnet be,
And have no business but dispensing round
Their magnanimities of sound,
Nor but in merriment begin a chase,
Nor but in merriment a quarrel.
O may she live like some green laurel
Rooted in one dear perpetual place.

My mind, because the minds that I have loved,
The sort of beauty that I have approved,
Prosper but little, has dried up of late,
Yet knows that to be choked with hate
May well be of all evil chances chief.
If there's no hatred in a mind
Assault and battery of the wind
Can never tear the linnet from the leaf.

An intellectual hatred is the worst,
So let her think opinions are accursed.
Have I not seen the loveliest woman born
Out of the mouth of Plenty's horn,
Because of her opinionated mind
Barter that horn and every good
By quiet natures understood
For an old bellows full of angry wind?

Considering that, all hatred driven hence,
The soul recovers radical innocence
And learns at last that it is self-delighting,
Self-appeasing, self-affrighting,
And that its own sweet will is Heaven's will;
She can, though every face should scowl
And every windy quarter howl
Or every bellows burst, be happy still.

And may her bridegroom bring her to a house
Where all's accustomed, ceremonious;
For arrogance and hatred are the wares
Peddled in the thoroughfares.
How but in custom and in ceremony
Are innocence and beauty born?
Ceremony's a name for the rich horn,
And custom for the spreading laurel tree.

Lapis Lazuli

I have heard that hysterical women say
They are sick of the palette and fiddle-bow,
Of poets that are always gay,
For everybody knows or else should know
That if nothing drastic is done
Aeroplane and Zeppelin will come out,
Pitch like King Billy bomb-balls in
Until the town lie beaten flat.

All perform their tragic play,
There struts Hamlet, there is Lear,
That's Ophelia, that Cordelia;
Yet they, should the last scene be there,
The great stage curtain about to drop,
If worthy their prominent part in the play,
Do not break up their lines to weep.
They know that Hamlet and Lear are gay;
Gaiety transfiguring all that dread.
All men have aimed at, found and lost;
Black out; Heaven blazing into the head:
Tragedy wrought to its uttermost.
Though Hamlet rambles and Lear rages,
And all the drop-scenes drop at once
Upon a hundred thousand stages,
It cannot grow by an inch or an ounce.

On their own feet they came, or on shipboard,
Camel-back; horseback, ass-back, mule-back,
Old civilisations put to the sword.
Then they and their wisdom went to rack:
No handiwork of Callimachus,

Who handled marble as if it were bronze,
Made draperies that seemed to rise
When sea-wind swept the corner, stands;
His long lamp-chimney shaped like the stem
Of a slender palm, stood but a day;
All things fall and are built again,
And those that build them again are gay.

Two Chinamen, behind them a third,
Are carved in lapis lazuli,
Over them flies a long-legged bird,
A symbol of longevity;
The third, doubtless a serving-man,
Carries a musical instrument.

Every discoloration of the stone,
Every accidental crack or dent,
Seems a water-course or an avalanche,
Or lofty slope where it still snows
Though doubtless plum or cherry-branch
Sweetens the little half-way house
Those Chinamen climb towards, and I
Delight to imagine them seated there;
There, on the mountain and the sky,
On all the tragic scene they stare.
One asks for mournful melodies;
Accomplished fingers begin to play.
Their eyes mid many wrinkles, their eyes,
Their ancient, glittering eyes, are gay.

Sweet Dancer

The girl goes dancing there
On the leaf-sown, new-mown, smooth
Grass plot of the garden;
Escaped from bitter youth,
Escaped out of her crowd,
Or out of her black cloud.
Ah, dancer, ah, sweet dancer!

If strange men come from the house
To lead her away, do not say
That she is happy being crazy;
Lead them gently astray;
Let her finish her dance,
Let her finish her dance.
Ah, dancer, ah, sweet dancer!

An Acre of Grass

Picture and book remain,
An acre of green grass
For air and exercise,
Now strength of body goes;
Midnight, an old house
Where nothing stirs but a mouse.

My temptation is quiet.
Here at life's end
Neither loose imagination,
Nor the mill of the mind
Consuming its rag and bone,
Can make the truth known.

Grant me an old man's frenzy,
Myself must I remake
Till I am Timon and Lear
Or that William Blake
Who beat upon the wall
Till Truth obeyed his call;

A mind Michael Angelo knew
That can pierce the clouds,
Or inspired by frenzy
Shake the dead in their shrouds;
Forgotten else by mankind,
An old man's eagle mind.

What Then?

His chosen comrades thought at school
He must grow a famous man;
He thought the same and lived by rule,
All his twenties crammed with toil;
'What then?' sang Plato's ghost. 'What then?'

Everything he wrote was read,
After certain years he won
Sufficient money for his need,
Friends that have been friends indeed;
'What then?' sang Plato's ghost. 'What then?'

All his happier dreams came true –
A small old house, wife, daughter, son,
Grounds where plum and cabbage grew,
Poets and Wits about him drew;
'What then?' sang Plato's ghost. 'What then?'

'The work is done,' grown old he thought,
'According to my boyish plan;
Let the fools rage, I swerved in naught,
Something to perfection brought';
But louder sang that ghost, 'What then?'

The Curse of Cromwell

You ask what I have found, and far and wide I go:
Nothing but Cromwell's house and Cromwell's murderous
        crew,
The lovers and the dancers are beaten into the clay,
And the tall men and the swordsmen and the horsemen,
        where are they?
And there is an old beggar wandering in his pride —
His fathers served their fathers before Christ was crucified.
            O what of that, O what of that,
            What is there left to say?

All neighbourly content and easy talk are gone,
But there's no good complaining, for money's rant is on.
He that's mounting up must on his neighbour mount,
And we and all the Muses are things of no account.
They have schooling of their own, but I pass their
        schooling by,
What can they know that we know that know the time
        to die?
            O what of that, O what of that,
            What is there left to say?

But there's another knowledge that my heart destroys,
As the fox in the old fable destroyed the Spartan boy's
Because it proves that things both can and cannot be;
That the swordsmen and the ladies can still keep company,
Can pay the poet for a verse and hear the fiddle sound,
That I am still their servant though all are underground.
            O what of that, O what of that,
            What is there left to say?

I came on a great house in the middle of the night,
Its open lighted doorway and its windows all alight,
And all my friends were there and made me welcome too;
But I woke in an old ruin that the winds howled through;
And when I pay attention I must out and walk
Among the dogs and horses that understand my talk.

> *O what of that, O what of that,*
> *What is there left to say?*

Roger Casement

I say that Roger Casement
Did what he had to do.
He died upon the gallows,
But that is nothing new.

Afraid they might be beaten
Before the bench of Time,
They turned a trick by forgery
And blackened his good name.

A perjurer stood ready
To prove their forgery true;
They gave it out to all the world,
And that is something new;

For Spring Rice had to whisper it,
Being their Ambassador,
And then the speakers got it
And writers by the score.

Come Tom and Dick, come all the troop
That cried it far and wide,
Come from the forger and his desk,
Desert the perjurer's side;

Come speak your bit in public
That some amends be made
To this most gallant gentleman
That is in quicklime laid.

The Ghost of Roger Casement

O what has made that sudden noise?
What on the threshold stands?
It never crossed the sea because
John Bull and the sea are friends;
But this is not the old sea
Nor this the old seashore.
What gave that roar of mockery,
That roar in the sea's roar?
The ghost of Roger Casement
Is beating on the door.

John Bull has stood for Parliament,
A dog must have his day,
The country thinks no end of him,
For he knows how to say,
At a beanfeast or a banquet,
That all must hang their trust
Upon the British Empire,
Upon the Church of Christ.
The ghost of Roger Casement
Is beating on the door.

John Bull has gone to India
And all must pay him heed,
For histories are there to prove
That none of another breed
Has had a like inheritance,
Or sucked such milk as he,
And there's no luck about a house
If it lack honesty.

The ghost of Roger Casement
Is beating on the door.

I poked about a village church
And found his family tomb
And copied out what I could read
In that religious gloom;
Found many a famous man there;
But fame and virtue rot.
Draw round, beloved and bitter men,
Draw round and raise a shout;
The ghost of Roger Casement
Is beating on the door.

The Wild Old Wicked Man

'Because I am mad about women
I am mad about the hills,'
Said that wild old wicked man
Who travels where God wills.
'Not to die on the straw at home.
Those hands to close these eyes,
That is all I ask, my dear,
From the old man in the skies.
                    Daybreak and a candle-end.

'Kind are all your words, my dear,
Do not the rest withhold.
Who can know the year, my dear,
when an old man's blood grows cold?
I have what no young man can have
Because he loves too much.
Words I have that can pierce the heart,
But what can he do but touch?'
                    Daybreak and a candle-end.

Then said she to that wild old man,
His stout stick under his hand,
'Love to give or to withhold
Is not at my command.
I gave it all to an older man:
That old man in the skies.
Hands that are busy with His beads
Can never close those eyes.'
                    Daybreak and a candle-end.

'Go your ways, O go your ways,
I choose another mark,
Girls down on the seashore
Who understand the dark;
Bawdy talk for the fishermen;
A dance for the fisher-lads;
When dark hangs upon the water
They turn down their beds.
                    Daybreak and a candle-end.

'A young man in the dark am I,
But a wild old man in the light,
That can make a cat laugh, or
Can touch by mother wit
Things hid in their marrow-bones
From time long passed away,
Hid from all those warty lads
That by their bodies lay.
                    Daybreak and a candle-end.

'All men live in suffering,
I know as few can know,
Whether they take the upper road
Or stay content on the low,
Rower bent in his row-boat
Or weaver bent at his loom,
Horseman erect upon horseback
Or child hid in the womb.
                    Daybreak and a candle-end.

'That some stream of lightning
From the old man in the skies
Can burn out that suffering

No right-taught man denies.
But a coarse old man am I,
I choose the second-best,
I forget it all awhile
Upon a woman's breast.'

Daybreak and a candle-end.

A Drunken Man's Praise of Sobriety

Come swish around, my pretty punk,
And keep me dancing still
That I may stay a sober man
Although I drink my fill.
Sobriety is a jewel
That I do much adore;
And therefore keep me dancing
Though drunkards lie and snore.
O mind your feet, O mind your feet,
Keep dancing like a wave,
And under every dancer
A dead man in his grave.
No ups and downs, my pretty,
A mermaid, not a punk;
A drunkard is a dead man,
And all dead men are drunk.

Colonel Martin

The Colonel went out sailing,
He spoke with Turk and Jew,
With Christian and with Infidel,
For all tongues he knew.
'O what's a wifeless man?' said he,
And he came sailing home.
He rose the latch and went upstairs
And found an empty room.
The Colonel went out sailing.

'I kept her much in the country
And she was much alone,
And though she may be there,' he said,
'She may be in the town.
She may be all alone there,
For who can say?' he said.
'I think that I shall find her
In a young man's bed.'
The Colonel went out sailing.

The Colonel met a pedlar,
Agreed their clothes to swop,
And bought the grandest jewelry
In a Galway shop,
Instead of thread and needle
Put jewelry in the pack,
Bound a thong about his hand,
Hitched it on his back.
The Colonel went out sailing.

The Colonel knocked on the rich man's door,
'I am sorry,' said the maid,
'My mistress cannot see these things,
But she is still abed,
And never have I looked upon
Jewelry so grand.'
'Take all to your mistress,'
And he laid them on her hand.
The Colonel went out sailing.

And he went in and she went on
And both climbed up the stair,
And O he was a clever man,
For he his slippers wore.
And when they came to the top stair
He ran on ahead,
His wife he found and the rich man
In the comfort of a bed.
The Colonel went out sailing.

The Judge at the Assize Court,
When he heard that story told,
Awarded him for damages
Three kegs of gold.
The Colonel said to Tom his man,
'Harness an ass and cart,
Carry the gold about the town,
Throw it in every part.'
The Colonel went out sailing.

And there at all street-corners
A man with a pistol stood,
And the rich man had paid them well

To shoot the Colonel dead;
But they threw down their pistols
And all men heard them swear
That they could never shoot a man
Did all that for the poor.
The Colonel went out sailing.

'And did you keep no gold, Tom?
You had three kegs,' said he.
'I never thought of that, sir.'
'Then want before you die.'
And want he did; for my own grand-dad
Saw the story's end,
And Tom make out a living
From the seaweed on the strand.
The Colonel went out sailing.

Are You Content?

I call on those that call me son,
Grandson, or great-grandson,
On uncles, aunts, great-uncles or great-aunts,
To judge what I have done.
Have I, that put it into words,
Spoilt what old loins have sent?
Eyes spiritualised by death can judge,
I cannot, but I am not content.

He that in Sligo at Drumcliff
Set up the old stone Cross,
That red-headed rector in County Down,
A good man on a horse,
Sandymount Corbets, that notable man
Old William Pollexfen,
The smuggler Middleton, Butlers far back,
Half legendary men.

Infirm and aged I might stay
In some good company,
I who have always hated work,
Smiling at the sea,
Or demonstrate in my own life
What Robert Browning meant
By an old hunter talking with Gods;
But I am not content.

Index of First Lines